Saturday Ga

Visit the author's website:

www.garytwynam.com

Saturday Gambler

(Introduction to 2016 version)

Introduction

(Postscript to 2016 version)

(Update to Introduction 2016)

This book was written in the winter of 2001/2002. I wrote it in four weeks when there was little racing to distract me, and in a rush to get my thoughts down.

I then set about getting published – not having a clue how to do so. Via theracingforum I managed to get Alan Potts to read it. At that time Alan was the best-known mainstream grounded professional gambler. By grounded I mean he was a believable character. He wasn't one of those larger-than-life big-staking punters who blow in each decade, hogging the limelight before blowing up spectacularly with massive debts. Alan had also published two superb books on gambling on the horses, both of which I recommend more highly than this one. We met at Kempton racecourse where he had a horse running.

It was fascinating to meet a bona fide professional gambler close-up, and in his natural habitat. He would talk about horses going back years and could tell you the ratings they ran off. At one time I mentioned Desert Orchid breaking poor old little Yahoos' heart in the Gold cup and he said, yes, except Yahoo won his next and only race off 176 at Aintree, and then won a bunch of point to points.

He was very helpful to me, endorsed the book, gave me the name of a publisher and promised me a quote to adorn the cover. He even gave us a tip before he left to greet his horse in the paddock. Just imagine what you would do if a bona fide professional gambler had taken time out of his day to see you, had been incredibly helpful and had left you with a tip for a horse running elsewhere along with a compelling analysis as to why the price seemed generous. I wrote a silly haiku about what me and my mate did.

At The Races (Kempton)

We met Alan Potts
He gave us a winning tip
We didn't back it

Anyway, the book was about to be published and then it wasn't for details too long and boring to explore here, and the publisher disappeared for ever, and the book has lain dormant in a laptop file ever since. Well actually, not strictly true. I did give it to three people. One of them was the friend who came to Kempton with me to meet Alan Potts. He was just getting into betting and read the book, took all of its advice on board, started his own betting fund and has been doing it ever since. Profitably. There have been some losing years but his fund has grown steadily and surely, which I take as at least some sort of endorsement of the book.

Another person I met online had a website called Slippery Toad, which logged his attempt to become a professional gambler. He read every book he could get his hands on, and really took to mine for some reason. I have used his endorsement on the cover, for he is now a successful professional gambler and has contacted me a number of times over the years to encourage me to finally publish the book. The third person was less successful. He just likes a punt.

So, what happened to my gambling in the intervening years? Well, after the book was published I had a number of successful years gambling – very nearly full-time for a number of them. When I say highly successful I mean I earnt at least the annual average salary at the time – tax-free. That was what I was aiming for and that was what I achieved.

But as a codicil to that I did not make this money grinding out a simple weekly, monthly profit from horse racing. For starters a lot, if not most, of my profits came from reality TV betting and similar.

This only really started to be a key opportunity after the book was written and I was around at the right time to take optimum advantage. With the horses I had more of a rollercoaster, and was unquestionably helped by three trebles over the years which each returned 5 figures. The biggest was 22k.

When I was writing the book my bets were actually modest, both in real terms and as a percentage of my betting bank. A normal win single was £30 and half a per cent of my bank. At my height I was betting £500 for a single win as 1 per cent of my bank. I say "at the height" and that should be a clue.

Things changed in 2007. Not least because we moved from Tooting to Shropshire, and not least because we flooded very soon afterwards, and suffered other unsettlements. This combined with a changing market – reality TV markets were becoming more mature and sensible and where the value in horse races was to be found seemed to be changing – meant my edge disappeared and, slowly but surely, over the next three years did my bank. I was able to take income along the way, but by 2010 the writing was on the wall.

To be honest I was heartbroken. Still, I turned my attentions to other things – even had a novel published – and went back to fun – ie mug-punting for a few years. Then two years ago I found a new edge in novice jumps races and similar uncompetitive lower class races. I started to quietly exploit this as best I could with no real starting bank to speak of. In 2015 I made a profit in each and every month and paid most of it straight out in dividends. 2016 has not been as profitable but the edge remains.

So, there we are.

I was at a loose end in the summer of 2016 and thought I should do something with all the unpublished material I have hanging around. Sweep them all together and put them up on my website and

Amazon for sale alongside the other more properly published stuff. So, I read this through. Oh lord – so much of it is out of date – the game, the market, technology has moved on. And so much of my approach has changed. And I certainly didn't have the energy for a complete re-write of a book no-one will buy. But I liked some of it. It made me smile, and I recognised it as still being a useful primer for eager starters. A friend's son was starting to gamble – on football – and I started to help him gamble better, and realised how much we take for granted – those of us who have been doing it for years. There's a simplicity about the book that still holds true. And also I liked the historical record – a snapshot of one person's betting approach at a particular time in history.

So I settled on a fudge, as is my way. I wouldn't re-write it, but I would write this introduction and provide a short extra chapter at the end of the book – as an update, critique and comment on what might or might not still be valid.

If three people buy it, I'll be happy. If two of them went on to success as per first time around, I'd be over the moon.

Introduction

Picking winners is easy (apparently). Making money from them is altogether harder. In fact, listening to most people's responses when I tell them I'm a semi-professional gambler, impossible. Succeeding at doing something so difficult is very satisfying. And a constant battle. To be successful at gambling you need to be prepared for your bets to lose. Most of the time.

You also need to trust your own opinion, and be able to fly in the face of the majority. This will include ignoring public opinion that says such and such a horse is a stone-cold bonking certainty for the big race, and lumping your money on the horse the Channel 4 commentators are laughing about in the pre-race waffle.

If you do become successful it will also include living with the fact that hardly anyone will believe you. Often people have just immediately assumed I must be a complete waster, before going on to point out knowingly that it's a mug's game, and looking at my wife with pity in their eyes for her being stuck with such a sad deluded loser.

Other folk will share your interest and enjoyment, if not necessarily your success. Often they too will wink conspiratorially at you, thinking you're just having a bit of harmless fun, like them. And sometimes, on a bad day, you'll agree with them. And when you're on a thirty bet losing streak, stretching back a month or more, you'll also be muttering it's a mug's game.

It took me ten years of learning to get to the stage where I felt I could make money from gambling, and another five years to prove it to the point where I felt able to write this book. Which isn't to say it could all go wrong tomorrow. If nothing else, this game keeps you humble.

I'm lucky enough to have a few close friends who have invested in a gambling fund, which we run exactly like a unit trust. We have a lot of fun along the way, and one of them has more than doubled his money over the last few years. I'm pretty proud of that.

And I although I do love racing, it's the gambling that's at the core of that love. There was one of those lists in the Sunday Observer a while back where they listed the top 10 racehorses of all time. I enjoyed it, but it meant little to me. Of course, I love the big races, the big occasions, a sense of having seen greatness. But my top 10 racehorses were completely different animals. They were ones that had won fairly big races for sure, but they had won them at nice prices, with enough of my money on them for it to matter.

In recent years, my favourite horses would include:

What's Up Boys   14/1, 14/1 and 40/1.
Kingsmark   25/1
Compton Admiral 25/1
Folly Road   100/1 (2nd)
Happy Diamond   8/1, 8/1, 8/1
Landing Light   16/1

Going further back to the all-time favourites I could add
Bradbury Star
Remittance man
Atone
Barathea

They all won me money after I'd spent time looking through the options, and had decided they represented the best bet. I guess I'm contrary and opinionated by nature, but that's the key thrill of gambling to me, being in the minority but proven right. And proven right in hard cash. What simpler measure of success could there be?

I mainly place bets over the phone or internet these days. I find it easier, quicker, and less frightening than counting out notes. On the other hand, it means I miss the thrill of going to the betting shop to pick up a huge wad of cash and then running all the way home through pure adrenaline, and the fear of being mugged.

So, for years now I've been battling away trying to make a profit from studying horse-racing (and other sports). And this book is the culmination of that battle so far. It's a great time to be a gambler. Tax-free gambling allows a real opportunity for increased profits. Don't make the mistake of thinking this book will suddenly make you rich, because it won't. But, I do believe it can help you improve your returns.

I owe a debt to many writers before me, for the insights they have provided. Twenty years ago, I read a book by Clive Holt called 'Be a Successful Punter' and that is still a fine introduction. But it was Nick Mordin that changed my betting life, with the brilliant 'Betting for a Living'. He also introduced me to all the American authors like Beyer and Quinn, who had so influenced him. Mark Coton's work on 'value' and Alan Potts' notes as a full-time professional both added depth to my own approach.

If I repeat any of their advice, or it seems that I have stolen their words, it will be because they have influenced me to the point where some of their ways are now a fundamental part of my method. I hope they take that as a compliment. That said, I believe I have my own approach. This book will serve as a standalone manual for people who haven't read the above, and as an additional tool for those who have.

It was Andy Beyer who split gambling into three skills: Picking winners, money management, and mind management. I mainly agree, but prefer to divide 'picking winners' into two elements –

shortlisting possible winners, and choosing the right bet. This book tracks through these 4 skills, tackling each of them in order.

Chapter 1 – Getting started

"Put more money on the horses that win, and less money on the horses that lose." *(Advice from one of the investors in my gambling fund)*

Some assumptions

I'm going to make some assumptions about you as a reader.

You have some experience of betting on horses, and probably other sports as well.

If you are fairly new to betting, don't worry. I may bamboozle you with jargon, or otherwise confuse you. However, if you follow the book step-by-step, chapter-by-chapter, you should do fine. At the very least it will be a crash-course on the fundamentals of betting on horses.

If you are really new, I strongly recommend you read either the Clive Holt book referred to in the introduction, or 'Braddock's Complete Guide to Horse Race Selection and Betting'.

Those of you who are experienced bettors are slightly different. If you are already sure that you make a profit from gambling, you'll no doubt be looking to this book less for its overall approach and more to uncover anything that can give you even more of edge. I hope you find something. If you 'break even', or lose over the long-term, I'd recommend having a go at following the book closely, rather than dipping into it.

Another assumption is that you're prepared to spend a couple of hours on a Saturday, or other major racing days, to 'study the form', and place your bets.

The last assumption is that you're willing to buy the Racing Post on race day, and preferably the Racing Post Weekender every Wednesday. I won't be asking you to do anything more onerous or expensive than that. However, if you think I'm going to show you how to be a millionaire from some cunning system devised around the spotlighted horses in the Sun or Mirror, tough.

The final thing to say is that the book is about an approach to betting. As will become clear, just because you follow this approach does not mean you will end up making the same bets as me. The book is about having a structured methodology, not about applying a rigid system.

Requirements

1. A dedicated betting bank account.
    It's essential that you keep your gambling bank separate from your other money (assuming you have any). We'll see why in a later chapter. You could of course use a cash bank for lesser sums. I will cover how much you should have in your bank in some detail in a later chapter.

2. Betting accounts
    You will need a lot of betting accounts. We will be taking early prices where beneficial. I tend to use the internet from habit, but shops and phone are also tax free these days. Be careful of the smaller bookies. I can't imagine anything worse than having a nice win and then not getting paid-out.

Take your time opening the accounts – wait and take advantage of all the lip-smacking offers each firm makes to new clients from time to time.

I have (mainly Switch) accounts with Ladbrokes, Coral, William Hill, Tote, Blue Square, Sportingbet, Stanley, Paddy Power, Victor Chandler, Sporting Odds, Flutter.com and Sporting Index. I should really have more than one spread bet account, and probably even more accounts.

3. The Racing Post.
   I guess it would make sense to have it delivered. Personally, I like to go for a walk to the newsagents to blow away the cobwebs.

4. Racing Post Weekender
   Not essential, but really useful, as we'll see in Chapter 3. I treat it like a bible. It also makes the weekend seem that much closer when I buy it on a Wednesday lunch-time.

5. An A4 size notebook. I use spiral-bound ones.
   This should be thick enough to last a season, (at least 100 pages). Making notes is absolutely critical. Most books tell you to detail your bets and quite right too. But there is a lot more you could be doing, as we shall see.

6. Different coloured pens – red, black and blue, for me.

7. Access to the internet. Not essential, though I find it increasingly so. Some sites, such as oddschecker.co.uk, which compares prices from most bookies, are incredibly helpful. If not, access to teletext is at least something.

8. If you do have a PC, you'll be able to set up simple spreadsheets, to keep a record of your bets, and profit/loss.

Choosing the races to bet in.

In the early days I would approach this as follows: Saturday afternoon, duck into the nearest betting-shop. Look at the paper on the wall, and pick out the big race of the day. Pick a horse, usually the one with my favourite jockey on board, fill in a slip, take the price, and be on my way. Check on the result later. Scan the ranks of screens with a pretend uncaring smile on my face, throw losing slip on floor, and leave the shop cursing Ray Cochrane for being such a useless git.

In time, I became more sophisticated. I'd do a Yankee on the four TV races, then an each way lucky 15, or the placepot at the big meeting. Before long I was spending the afternoon in Ladbrokes having a bet in every race. And having a great time. But losing. It was around then that I started reading the books on gambling, and started betting more wisely.

And the first key element to betting wisely is deciding what races you should be betting in, and those you should avoid.

There is rather too much racing these days. In theory, you could bet on any race that takes your fancy. There's even wall-to-wall American racing every evening on satellite TV. And greyhounds from around the world. And a thousand other sports betting opportunities.

I prefer to be more selective. And I would urge you to do likewise. Let's stick to UK horse racing for now. One way would be to stick to TV races. This has a lot to recommend it. There will be a fair amount of coverage of the race in the papers, or on TV (Channel 4's Morning Line for example), and more importantly if you want to, you'll be able to enjoy both the build-up and the race live from the comfort of your home. After all, this book is about making a profit, but not about forfeiting all pleasure to do so.

There are a couple of downsides though. Often the TV races are the most competitive racing there are. In some races, any of 20 runners could conceivably win. Also, often the races have been done to death by the media, meaning any chance of finding some value has long since gone.

My approach to choosing races focuses more on the type of race. However, since I concentrate on the better racing you normally get at the top tracks on a Saturday, or at major mid-week meetings, they still tend to include most of the TV races.

Races I concentrate on

My major focus is on class. So I disregard almost all races below C class. Over the years I haven't been able to profit from lower class races. My approach to form study just doesn't work with the more unreliable lower-class horses. I also prefer races where there is going to be a range of early prices.

I avoid the types of races where I have no real record of profit, and concentrate on those areas where my methods do seem to work best. You'll need to find what races work best for you. At the start of each season I suggest you set yourself guidelines as to which races you are going to bet on and which races you are going to avoid.

On a normal Saturday, there will be two meetings where I may find bets. I turn to the main meeting and study the types of races, and put a line through any that don't suit. Usually I will be left with a few races at each meeting – say 5 in total, to study. Some Saturdays I can find myself with 10 potential races spread across 4 meetings, in which case I may be even more selective. On others, I might struggle to find more than a couple. That's when I can be tempted (usually wrongly) into tackling that tricky C Class Novice handicap hurdle with 25 unexposed runners. Betting because you need the action is a guaranteed road to penury. We'll look at how to deal with it later.

Having up to 11 races to consider will mean you need to get a crack on in the morning. Ideally, you want to have 'framed' your races by 10:30 to make sure you are in line to get the best prices. In winter, you need the whole thing done and dusted by the time of the first race of the day, which can be as early as 12:30. Having said that, if I'm honest I usually start about 9:30, and have usually placed all my bets by 1pm at the latest.

Let's take a typical Saturday and see what races I'd be short-listing.

Saturday December 8th 2001

Main meeting – Sandown
Race 1 Handicap Chase – Class C
Race 2 Novices Handicap Hurdle Class D
Race 3 Grade 2 Novices Chase (TV)
Race 4 Tingle Creek Chase Grade 1 (TV)
Race 5 Listed Handicap Hurdle (TV)
Race 6 Handicap Hurdle Class C (TV)

The only race I'd definitely throw out is Race 2 – a novices' handicap hurdle, even though it has fairly generous prize money. I've never done very well in in novice handicaps, and just a quick look at the entries suggests a fair few unexposed horses. The three graded races at the heart of the meeting are exactly what I like to bet on, and I'll concentrate on those. The races at the start and finish of the meeting are possible. Depending on the standard of racing elsewhere, I may decide to study them or may not. Of the two I much prefer the look of Race 1, a decent 2m4f chase, compared to the Race 6 – a handicap hurdle over 2m 6f where there maybe a lot of horses stepping up in trip.

Second Meeting - Chepstow
Race 1 Novices Selling Hurdle
Race 2 Handicap Chase Class C (TV)
Race 3 Handicap Hurdle Class B (TV)
Race 4 Handicap Chase Grade 2 (TV)
Race 5 Novice Chase Class D
Race 6 Maiden Hurdle Class D

Races 1 and 6 can go without a second's thought, and I'm looking forward to Races 3 and 4. Races 2 and 5 join the possible list.

Third Meeting – Wetherby
Race 1 Novices handicap Hurdle Class E
Race 2 Novices Chase Class D
Race 3 Handicap Chase Class B (TV)
Race 4 Novices Hurdle Class D
Race 5 Handicap Chase Class C
Race 6 Handicap Hurdle Class C (TV)

Race 3 is the only definite for the short-list, but Races 2, 5, and 6 join the short-list.

That leaves me with a total of 6 races to definitely study, and 7 possibles. I'd tackle the 6 races first, and then see how I felt.

What I actually ended up doing was as follows. At Sandown, I ended up only considering the 3 big races (3, 4 and 5). Both the C class races looked tricky, and full of horses I either hadn't heard of, or knew to be inconsistent. Race 6 was as expected full of horses unproven over the trip. It took me about a minute looking at each to decide they weren't for me. I studied each of the three big races, although in the end I didn't find a bet in Race 3.

At Chepstow, the two big races were fine. I did end up studying the C Class Handicap chase, and did end up having a bet in it, and wishing that I hadn't.

Wetherby's meeting was much less interesting than it may have first appeared. The races may have been C Class, but they were poor C Class, mainly full of D and E class horses. Despite the number of possible races it took me only a couple of minutes to end up concentrating on the main race.

So, I ended up studying the 6 certainties, but only one of the possibles. That would be typical of a day like this, where there are a lot of big races, and fair supporting cards. I find I will turn my noses up at the C Class races and concentrate on the really big races. On a quieter Saturday, or mid-week, I would be much more likely to take the time over the lower grade 'possible' races.

Chapter 2 - 'Circling' Horses

"She never made the same mistake again – she always made a different one instead." Wendy Cope

In the early days, I would follow particular horses. I couldn't help it really. I'd back a horse, it would win, so I'd back it again. It would lose. And again. And again. And again. Finally, I'd give up on the horse, just in time for it to bolt in at 33/1. It's a bit like all those people who do the lottery with the same numbers each week. It gets so they dare not do it for fear of that being the week the numbers come up.

I'd often reached the stage where I was backing three or more runners in the same race, all because they were my horses. And I had some great fun from it – Bradbury Star gave me some great memories – winning two Mackesons, and being second in photos in both the Sun Alliance Chase and the King George. But it was a quick route to poverty. I still have favourite horses, but am much more sensible about when and how to back them.

The first stage of picking winners is 'circling' all horses that have a chance of winning the race. This provides a short-list of possibles, all of which could form part of a potential bet.

What we need to do is work out which horses can win today given the conditions and which horses we believe we can effectively discard. My records show that over the last few years the horses that I have 'circled' consistently win 75% of the races. Obviously, that means I completely cock up (fall at the first fence as it were) with 25% of the races I study. However, this overall percentage is enough to give me an edge.

You will need to measure your own ability to find a short-list of winners.

It will depend to some extent on what proportion of horses in each race you are short-listing. Obviously, your strike-rate will be higher if you are shortlisting 6 horses out of 8, than if you are shortlisting 2 out of 8.

Once you've reduced the day's racing to a few manageable races, turn to the relevant form pages of the Racing Post. In doing so make no attempt to look at the prices for the race, or at any tipster information etc. It's critical that you look at the bare form with a detached eye. I'll repeat that again because it's so important. Make no attempt to look at the prices for the race, or at any tipster information etc. It's critical that you look at the bare form with a detached eye.

Take each horse in turn. The Racing Post form pages usually provide details as follows: weight, age, breeding, trainer, jockey, career placings, official rating, summary of career placings, plus prize money, details of each race won, summary of ability over a variety of conditions, and finally details of its last few outings.

The purpose of deciphering all this information is to decide if there is sufficient evidence that the horse cannot win given today's conditions. This is not a science. We probably wouldn't come up with the same short-list as each other. In fact, I could wait an hour, do it again, and probably come up with a slightly different list. Over time though I have found I can cross many horses off without much thought.

Your choice of races will have to be taken into account. It's much easier to delete horses where there is a lot of form available. You will probably now see the link between why I prefer studying the races I do, and why I avoid those races of unraced or lightly-raced horses. Where there is no compelling evidence to throw a horse out, I believe you have to keep it in.

Let's look at some of the reasons to chuck a horse out. I actually do my analysis on a horse-by-horse basis. However, to illustrate the process involved, I'll take you through the basic factors in turn.

Age

If a horse is 13 years old I cross it out. I can't remember the stats but I read something pointing out that 13 year olds hardly ever win. I can safely say that for the last few years I've been doing this none has won a race I've studied. That suggests they may still be able to pick up an egg and spoon around some gaff track, but aren't likely to win at a top track.

Also, remember that most horses go backwards. Older horses are likely to be in decline, younger ones still potentially improving. This in itself does not provide you with sufficient ammunition to cross a horse out, but it should make you look for signs of deteriorating form.

Strike-rate

Cross out any horse in a handicap that is a maiden. Again, this won't work at all levels of racing, but works well for top races.

Be prepared to cross out perennial losers. The Post provides details as follows – number of starts, and number of times the horse has finished 1st, 2nd or 3rd.

Let's take a few examples: These horses raced against each other on Friday November 30th 2001 at Newbury in a 2 mile C handicap hurdle race, £9,750 to the winner. Their previous hurdle starts were documented as follows:

Horse	Starts	1st	2nd	3rd
Abajany	10	0	1	2
Batswing	8	2	1	3
Carandrew	22	6	0	0
Haditovski	25	6	4	2
Iris Collonges	5	1	2	1
Jaguar	15	1	2	1
Marble Arch	9	2	2	2
Maximus	4	2	0	0
Reggie Buck	30	6	7	2
Summer Break	5	2	0	1
Victory Roll	9	3	0	1

Just from this I would be quite happy to cross out Abajany without a second's thought. There are enough horses here capable of winning races to believe Abajany will not be breaking his duck in this company. Of the rest, I roughly like to see a win rate of at least a quarter, and a win and place rate of 50%. Jaguar is the second horse I feel comfortable about deleting. I will be looking at Carandrew, Haditovski and Reggie Buck closely to try to find any patterns. The horses that have run less than 10 times all look like they could be improvers.

Class

One key question to ask is 'has the horse the class to win today's race?' Think about athletics for a moment. Distance is critical for top athletes, as we'll see when we look at the importance of distance for horses. However, no matter how much below the top class Linford Christie may have been at a trip such as say 800m, he still would have beaten a fat old selling plater such as me.

Horses often come up against the class barrier, equivalent to those steps up from being the best at school, to being best for county, to best for country, to best in Europe, to best in world. A horse that can dominate in F class, can't cope with the quicker pace, or slicker jumping required for C class. Some horses get caught between being too highly-rated to win handicaps, but not quite good enough to win pattern events, and so on. As another example, in football think of all those forwards who bang in goals for fun in the lower leagues, but can't step up a division. Or Premiership forwards who can't step up to international football.

There are two pieces of information that can give you a clue as to whether they have the class or not. The first is details of their previous winning performances. Ideally you want evidence of having won this class of race in the past. From our list 4 horses have won a C class race – Batswing, Haditovski, Marble Arch and Maximus.

Carandrew's 6 races were won around the gaff tracks – Folkestone, Exeter, Taunton etc at E and F class. He put together 4 wins on the bounce during summer racing, but his last two starts have been in higher company (B and C) and he's run unplaced both times. This is enough for me to put a line through his chances today.

With the remaining horses, it pays to look at their most recent performances. Another rule of thumb I've used with great success is that if a horse has run unplaced in a lower-class race on its previous start it has little chance of winning today. Don't apply this automatically, but it does provide a useful filter. In this race Iris Collonges has had two bad runs in novice chases, and is now reverting to hurdling. His third latest start he was unplaced in a class D hurdle at Bangor, and he ran behind Marble Arch prior to that. Again, I'm happy to oppose today.

Finally, Reggie Buck can also go. He has been running well in D class races and could possibly step up. But again, his winning has all been done around lesser tracks for little prize money, he's previously failed in C class and has run behind both Batswing and the already deleted Iris Collonges. Having said all that, on another day I may well have kept him in. Victory Roll, on the other hand stays in on the basis of its last two runnings when it won F class handicaps. The horse may well meet a class barrier today, and I suspect it will, but he's not proven to be up against it. This is an example of the important distinction I've been trying to make. We're looking for reasons to cross horses out. If we can't find a compelling reason to delete a horse from consideration, we must keep it in.

Distance

I have a lot of time for distance statistics. If anything, I probably over-rate it as a factor. Looking at Linford Christie again, he may have been the best in the world at 100m, but he usually struggled at the highest level at 200m. I find that distinction equates quite well to 5f and 6f. Except for one major point – a running-track is a running-track, but each course is different. Not only are the distances not exactly rigorously measured, but some sprint tracks are blisteringly quick (Epsom), whilst others pretty tough (Ascot).

Some horses can barely get 5 furlongs, but give them Goodwood on fast ground and they'll be OK. Other horses get caught between trips, and are suited by either a stiff 5 furlongs or an easy 6 furlongs. I've used 5 and 6 furlongs as an example, because the press often lumps them both together as 'sprint' distances, but whilst some horses excel at both, usually it is not so clear-cut.

The same is true of most other distances. As a further rule I don't like horses stepping down in distance. I do like horses stepping up massively in distance. Some trainers specialise at this – Mark Johnston on the flat and Martin Pipe over jumps in particular. However, the reason I tend to avoid those 3m hurdle races and 2m flat races is they are usually full of horses trying the trip for the first time. I haven't enough information to delete them from consideration, and so end up with too many circled horses to make a bet. I have often considered looking at breeding to help me, but until I add that to my armoury I will continue to be circumspect in such circumstances.

Looking at our remaining horses, over today's trip of 2 miles, Batswing has been placed 5/7, Haditovski 12/23, Marble Arch 6/10, Maximus 2/2, but Victory Roll 0/4. I could be tempted to cross Victory Roll out at this stage, and often I would cross him out. I'll keep him in though, as his last two victories were at Folkestone over 2m1.5 furlongs, in soft and heavy ground. That may equate fairly well to Newbury on good going.

Course

I find a horse's previous record at the course can be very useful. In fact, of the three modifiers, distance, course and going, previous course record is probably the best predictor of performance. The old adage *'horses for courses'* certainly has some substance.

There may be reasons for this other than the horse's suitability to the unique track and distance conditions. The horse may be local, and not like travelling. Or the trainer may believe the course suits, and so train it to win there rather than elsewhere – a self-fulfilling prophecy.

Often the course just suits the running style of the horse. For example, the horse Ice seems to love York. He is very hard to beat there if he gets an uncontested lead. York favours front-runners for some reason – (I suggest a combination of a prevailing tail-wind and a flat, if not slightly downhill finish) – and Ice can just keep sticking his neck out through the final furlong.

Of our qualifiers, only two have run over the course, with both Haditovski and Maximus winning their only previous start – Haditovski a similar handicap hurdle, and Maximus a decent novice hurdle. None of the others can be deleted. If a horse had run unplaced say 5 times over the course I may well delete. It would suggest either the course wasn't suitable, and/or that the horse may be there for a run rather than trying to win.

Going

I'll nail my colours to the mast now. I recognise that the going is an important factor, but I believe it is the most over-rated factor in the mind of the betting public and the racing media. It is about equal in the scheme of things to the distance and course records looked at above. Some folk, most notably the otherwise excellent Alastair Down of the Racing Post and Channel 4 would have you believe it's about the only factor.

Horses can have clear going preferences, and these patterns are usually obvious. However, most meetings take place on going that is neither very soft, nor very firm, and here I feel going preferences are much over-rated. I only pay close attention to the going for deletion purposes as follows:

(a) In extremes – from which I mean very soft/heavy at one extreme and firm/hard at the other.

(b)   Where the horse has a clear pattern – eg in 20 races placed 8/10 in races on soft, and 0/10 in races on good to firm.

I think trainers especially perpetuate the over-emphasis on going requirements, as it suits their own ends. What better excuse has a trainer got than to say the horse wasn't suited by the going. If you don't believe me save a copy of the Racing Post, and review the comments made by the trainers prior to the race and those made afterwards. You'll find that the comments on going preferences prior to the race have little bearing on the results. You'll also be amazed at how those stated going preferences seem to change race by race.

Our Newbury race is being run on good ground (with good/soft patches). That means we can only delete a horse if it has a marked preference for heavy or firm. All the horses left seem to have a slight preference for softer going, which makes today's conditions suitable enough.

Recent Form

If a horse hasn't won for a couple of years, cross it out. They can win, but not often at this level, and not often enough to worry about.

Also, see if the horse looks like it's struggling. Often horses are hurting somewhere, or just out of love with racing, but the trainers run it anyway. Horses that have been losing by miles over the previous few races, especially in similar company probably have something wrong with them.

However, always allow horses a warm-up run, or two. Some horses take a while to get fit.

Always forgive a horse one bad run. Mark Coton criticised himself in one of his books for looking too far back in a horse's form. I think that's a useful learning point. But the betting public is also notoriously fickle. A horse may have gone off a well-backed favourite and run appallingly. If the horse turns out again soon afterwards the public may well turn against the horse, even if once the latest run is forgiven, he is clearly the best horse in the race.

Our horses have all run OK in their previous starts. Marble Arch has been off the track for 6 months. If it was for a whole season I'd be tempted to cross it out unless it was trained by a top trainer who can get horses fit first time out. Maximus ran in a novice chase last time out, but unlike Iris Collonges ran respectably in hurdles before that. Batswing is stepping down in class, and Victory Roll stepping up after a couple of victories.

Conclusion

After looking at all these basic 'handicapping' factors we are left with 5 possible horses – Batswing, Haditovski, Marble Arch, Maximus and Victory Roll. Go to the racecard in the Racing Post and draw a circle around each of their race numbers. These are your 'circled' horses.

At this stage do a sanity check.
First look at the betting forecast. Normally, you will have picked most the market leaders.

The betting forecast for this race is
Batswing	3/1
Victory Roll	5/1
Carandrew	13/2
Haditovski	13/2
Reggie Buck	7/1

Iris Collonges	8/1
Marble Arch	10/1
Maximus	14/1
Jaguar	16/1
Abajany	20/1
Summer Break	20/1

If you've deleted any of the favourites you may want to re-check why. Either you've made a right royal rick-up, or you have uncovered a gem of a race, that will provide a host of betting opportunities. Best check you have the right one. If you have a complete outsider, also check you're not going to be tilting at windmills.

Then read the comments the race reader has given about each horse's chance. Use these as a further sanity check. They provide useful additional information, or can make you have a second look at the work you have done. The race-reader makes two interesting comments about this race. The first concerns Marble Arch. I am slightly worried by his lack of a run. But the race reader points out that the stable recently produced another horse to win at Cheltenham after a similar break.

The second concerns Reggie Buck. Remember, I have thrown this horse out on form grounds, but can imagine keeping him in if I did the study again. He is from the same stable as Haditovski and has been deserted by the stable jockey. I often back a stable's second string as we'll see but, in this instance, I take it as confirmation that he isn't good enough for this race.

After my sanity check I'm happy to have thrown out the outsiders, and also happy to have a couple of longer priced horses, and to have crossed-out some shorter priced horses. This is typical short-list for these sort of handicaps, and one that should provide us with a bet.

The above is the basic 'chore' that needs to be undertaken for each race you have short-listed for study. Don't feel you should only use the Racing Post. That is probably the minimum. Indeed, I'm sure many professional gamblers would be horrified that I don't use Timeform, or other more in-depth form books, and that I don't study a horse's entire racing history.

I subscribed to Timeform Perspective for a while, and collected all the weekly form supplements from the Weekender, but I never really profited from it. My biggest problem was I found that I was being pushed towards the favourites too readily. Timeform may be such an important source-book that it has too big a say in actually setting the market.

I also found it took too long and I would lose track or become bored half way through. This can happen to me with just the Racing Post. Sometimes I find a race isn't inspiring me, or I'm not getting a picture as to what's required to be considered a possible contender. In these circumstances, often where I find I'm just circling every horse in a 30 runner handicap, or circling no horses at all, I just give up and discard the race from consideration.

That's not to say that you can't circle every horse in the race. This will often be the case with smaller fields, and is perfectly acceptable. As an example, the last 15 races I have looked at, I have circled the following numbers of horses.

Race	Runners	Number circled	Circled won
1	20	7	N
2	20	2	Y
3	14	5	Y
4	13	4	Y
5	11	7	Y
6	9	5	Y
7	17	8	N
8	7	5	N!

9	14	11	Y
10	33	14	Y
11	9	2	Y
12	9	3	Y
13	7	6	Y
14	9	6	N
15	9	1	Y

When you've circled the horses for one race, go on to do all the other races on your short-list, before you look at any other details.

Chapter 3 – Alternative Handicapping

(The harder I practise the luckier I get)

When you've circled all your contenders in all your races you're ready for the next stage. I usually take a break at this stage (about 10:00), and make myself some toast and coffee. This is because I'm a boring anorak who takes pleasure in habit.

It's time for the next stage. So far, you've done what any half-decent gambler would have done, considered the basics, and come up with your contenders.

That used to be all I'd do. My next step would be to look at the prices and back a combination of the horse that most caught my eye, or the price I liked the best. Or I'd do combination forecasts if I'd only circled three or four horses, or the placepot, and so on.

And alongside these I'd do 'systems' bets. These were bets based on systems I'd picked up from books, or articles in the late lamented Odds On Magazine, or ones I'd devised myself.

One example was Nick Mordin's juvenile hurdler system. Back a horse that ran its first ever hurdle outing after November at a Grade 1 track and finished first or second. I had a lot of success with that for a while. But there were many more where that came from, usually less successful.

Effectively, I was following two separate approaches to betting. The first was based on normal form factors, and the second on what we'll call 'alternative' factors, or systems. What I wasn't doing was linking the two. With time, I came to realise that I could use the alternative factors as supplementary information to sit along-side the basic form factors.

The rest of this chapter will look at the alternative factors I currently use. I don't see that there's any limit to the factors you can come up with. Certainly, I am always adding and deleting factors, and always on the look-out for new ones.

Currently, I'm keen to get a greater knowledge of breeding, and sectional timing. And if there's one thing I tend to think of as the last critical factor, it would be the effect of the wind, particularly at those wide-open flat tracks like Newmarket and York. I'd love to find a way to incorporate that into my betting strategy.

Most of the ideas that follow have stood the test of time for me. and I tend to consider them 'core' factors these days. At the end, I'll add other ideas that I don't currently follow, but have done in the past, or could imagine myself studying further in the future.

What we're aiming to do is to build up a picture on our race-card of each of our circled horse's strengths and weaknesses today.

Trainer Form (circle trainer's name)

There was a time when I was obsessed by trainers, to the exclusion of virtually everything else, including the horses themselves. I continue to take a keen interest in the trainer but have now harnessed that interest within a more sensible framework.

One incredibly useful table in each day's Racing Post is the one close to the middle detailing how each trainer has done with their runners over the previous couple of weeks.

There are two things to note. Whether the trainer is bang in form, or whether the trainer's plainly got a problem in their yard.

We're not interested in every trainer, only the ones that train our circled horses. Look at the first race you have studied, look at the first horse you have circled and look up its trainer's record.

The information looks as follows

Trainer	last 14 days		
	Win	Place	Run
H Knight	12	8	33
W Jarvis	1	2	3
R Alner	4	3	20
M Chapman	0	0	21
H Daly	1	3	22
N Twiston-Davies	0	4	32

You need to take a view. There are no cast-iron rules, and you'll get a feel for it over time. Also, because you'll be looking at this table at least once a week, you'll begin to notice patterns and waves of form. For the top yards, I like to see a healthy win strike-rate, and an overall win and place rate of 50%. I've used this as a yard-stick for years now, and was pleased to see Mark Johnston unwittingly endorse it in his column in the Racing Post, where he said that he looked for a 50% runners to places ratio as a sign that his yard was in good health.

From the above you can see that Henrietta Knight's horses are flying. They have a great win-rate, and well over 50% win or place. She also had a winner yesterday. Jarvis is harder to fathom. He certainly seems to be doing well, but is running too few horses to be so confident. Given my past knowledge of his horses I'd be happy to give him the thumbs up as well. Alner is neither hot nor cold.

Where I believe a trainer is bang in form I circle the trainer's name in the race-card. That runner will now have a circle around its number and a circle around the trainer's name.

Where the trainer is clearly out of form, I would put a cross through the trainer's name. I have grown more careful with this over the years. I found that quite a few horses were winning despite their trainers being supposedly out of form, and it was costing me. I nearly dropped it as a factor.

Further study though showed that it was usually smaller trainers I was tripping up on. These trainers often only have a few horses, and often a few bad horses, and one good one, and I was letting the bad ones get in the way of the chances of the stable star. They also don't have enough runners to be statistically reliable. What is still interesting is where the bigger yards seem clearly out of form. A large trainer without a win for a few weeks may well have problems. If you have evidence of fancied runner running poorly, all the better. In terms of the poor performers above I'd be keen to cross-out Twiston-Davies, but would ignore Chapman and Daly.

Looking at the chart at least once a week, you will begin to get a good feel for trainers coming in and going out of form. The information is particularly useful in March and April on the flat, and October and November over the jumps, when the fitness of the horses is most open to doubt.

The Racing Post Weekender has another table which looks at the Top Jumps/Flat Trainers in Britain. This gives an overall strike rate for the season. The top yards will be above 20% wins to runs. It also has a useful figure showing the strike-rate for runners first time out. If I was looking at a race with a few unraced runners I would utilise this table as well, generally using 20% as worthy of a plus mark, and 5% or less worthy of a black mark.

Go through all your circled horses in all races. When you've finished, a few will have the trainer's name circled, a few will have the trainer's name crossed out, and the majority will be untouched.

Trainer Course Form (TRC)

I'm a great believer in this. Trainers have their favourite courses. And they tend to repeat what they have done in previous years. They'll introduce their best young horse in the same race as they have done successfully in previous years.

This is really useful. There are two tables that provide the relevant information. In the Racing Post there will be a table covering the top trainers for the course, looking back at trainers' records over the last 5 years. Essentially, they divide the performance into age on the flat, (2 year olds, and 3 year olds plus), and into chases and hurdles on the jumps.

The key figure to look for would be a strike-rate of over 20% in either category. This should be a percentage based on a large sample. For example, Martin Pipe currently has a strike-rate of 31% for his hurdlers at Newbury - 22/71 runners. That's pretty phenomenal. J Mackie also has a formidable strike-rate with his hurdlers at Newbury, a magnificent 33%. However, this is based on 3 runners and 1 winner. That's meaningless.

Be extra careful about small totals, where it could be a blip caused by one horse winning a string of races at the course.

On the down-side have a look at trainers with a rotten course record. Again, we are looking at clear evidence. For example, at Newbury Robert Alner has a strike rate of 4%, 1 winner from 23 runners. That does not inspire confidence in me for his runners' chances. Hobbs' record with hurdlers at Newbury is even more remarkable. 1/44, yet he has a perfectly respectable 5/28 for his chasers.

If the horse I was looking at was running in a hurdle and trained by Pipe I would write TRC against the horse.

On the other hand, if the circled horse I was looking at was in a hurdle race and trained by Hobbs, I would write TRC against the horse, and put a cross through TRC to signify a potential problem. I would also ask myself if there were any reason to think the horse may be not entirely trying today. For example, is it the horse's first run for a long time, or is it preparing for another race. One pointer to this may be a double-check as to the distance the horse is running over – a favourite losing-ploy of trainers is to run a horse over a wrong distance.

The Weekender often includes a similar training table. This one covers about 13 years worth of form (which may be too long on the one hand, but gives a larger statistical base on the other). It also divides the racing into more categories, dividing between handicaps and non handicaps. The same principles apply. Where possible I look at both tables before deciding on good and bad marks.

One extra part of this table that I like a lot is a breakdown of trainer's performance over the course, during the month in question. As I said many trainers repeat their patterns year after year, aiming their best horses at the same sorts of races. This means they will often target certain meetings, and this table can provide an indication of this.

Stable to follow *(StF)*

I've always found it useful to pick a stable for the coming season. This is seldom a large stable that has too many runners to fathom, nor one that is already over-bet by the public (so certainly not Martin Pipe's). Nor is it a small stable with infrequent runners in the big races. Small up and coming yards often work well, or one where you are beginning to notice patterns.

In the past, on the flat I've followed Geoff Wragg several times, Ed Dunlop and Mark Johnston. The latter one is probably too large, but I found I was uncovering some patterns in how he placed his horses that I liked, and ended up having my most successful season ever in the 2000 flat season, mainly from anticipating his winners. In successive years, even if you have stopped following the trainer you will find you have an enduring appreciation of their methods.

Over the jumps, I have kept keen eyes on Charlie Egerton, Venetia Williams and Henrietta Knight. Mark Pitman strikes me as one that would be good to follow right now. This jumps season (2001/2002) is a couple of months old as I write and I don't have a stable to follow at the moment, but I may yet adopt one.

Your starting-point would be the 'stable tour' articles weekly in the Post and the Weekender, where they visit a stable and the trainer talks about their hopes for their main horses, and provide statistics about the trainer's past performances. Try to imagine you are in charge, get to follow through the logic behind the race-planning, the jockey choices etc. See where the profits are made, work out when the horses are really trying, and so on. You should find you are in a great position to highlight horses as having a great chance or not for that stable.

Of course, I'm not talking about blindly following the stable's fortunes. That would be pointless and costly.

Horses to follow *(HtF)*

Similar to the above I like to choose NO MORE THAN 5 horses at the start of the season, and imagine they are my own. I do this more for jumps racing than for the flat, where horses are only around for five minutes. I own and train them. Where would I place them, when would they be having a prep race etc. In adopting them I follow all information about them. And as with the above I only use this information as supplementary handicapping information. Do not follow these horses blindly. Of course, as they are your favourites you do need to be aware that you may have to waste the odd tenner here or there, as you become so attached to them, but we will cover that in a later chapter.

My jumps horses for 2000/2001 were:
What's Up Boys
Chives
Churchstanton

My jumps horses for 2001/2002 were:
What's Up Boys
Lord Noelie
Chives.
Narrow Water

Pace (P)

Pace really does make the race. It can be difficult to predict how a race is going to be run, but if you get it right it can be incredibly rewarding. The importance of pace applies to nearly all types of race, from a 5 furlong sprint to a long-distance chase.

As with class and distance I have learnt a lot about pace from watching athletics over the years. The men's 800m and 1500m have always seemed instructive. Watch them closely next time they are on TV. The time of the first lap for the 800m is critical to how the race will unfold.

If it's relatively slow, the field will pack up, before sprinting flat out for the last 200 metres. In this instance the athletes have two concerns. The first is to make sure they are not going to get blocked and denied a run at a critical moment. The second is that they need to be somewhere near the front when the sprint starts. Both concerns stem from the fact they've turned the race into a flat-out sprint over just 200m. Regardless of their best times over the full trip, they probably all run within a couple of tenths of a second to each other over 200m. If they are out the back when the sprint starts they would have to be much faster sprinters than the others to win. If they get blocked, or forced wide round the last bend those lost tenths of seconds will be the difference between winning and losing. Bad luck stories abound. Occasionally a runner can actually come from last to first, even off a slow pace such is their speed, but they are eye-catching exceptions.

You see this all the time in racing. The jockeys set off at a crawl, and then get serious 2–3 furlongs from home. And exactly the same thing happens as happens in athletics – tight finishes, bumping and barging, your horse trapped behind a wall of horses and a huge advantage to the horses that get first run. Predicting that a race will be slowly run and that a certain horse is sure to be at the front when the taps are turned on, can be highly lucrative.

Another type of pace is what I call Steve Cram pace. In the 1500m, Steve didn't have the sprint finish of some of his rivals. His trick was to set or follow a decent pace until the last 400 to 600 metres, and then kick on and wind up the pace from the front. He'd usually have the field at full stretch down the back straight, and kick on into the home turn. If someone could lay up behind him, and follow his pace, they could out-kick him close home, but, until his declining years, they had to be a bit special to do so.

Again, you see this a lot in racing. One horse is allowed to dominate, sometimes poaching a healthy lead. You often see the jockey giving them a breather around the last bend, allowing the other horses to get close, and then immediately stepping on the gas coming out of the bend, and pulling away. Tony McCoy does something similar at Cheltenham, where he often tries to poach a lead coming down the hill, still a long way from home. Willie Ryan stole the Derby on Benny the Dip in exactly that fashion.

The jockey needs to have a good clock in their head to be able to front-run without going off too fast too early. It's worth noting jockeys who seem to have a good clock – Steve Cauthen was the master for me. Ones I'd commend from the last couple of seasons would be Darryll Holland, Richard Hughes, Frankie, Jimmy Fortune, plus Jimmy McCarthy over the jumps.

Another type of pace in athletics is the one usually set by pacemakers when a great runner is going for a world record. This is supposed to guarantee there is no shock and that class imposes itself. I can't remember a time when a pacemaker actually won an athletics race, but it does happen in racing. Sometimes the 'class' horses lay too far off the pacemaker, and fail to reel him in.

The final type of extreme pace is when the field goes off too quickly. Again, you see this in 800m races. The commentators exclaim as the field passes the bell in a ridiculous time, the field is stretched-out down the back straight, they tighten up on the home bend, and someone comes from the rear to cut their rivals down in the home straight.

Again, this is very common in horse racing. Where two or more jockeys are determined to get their horses to the front in the early stages, they can go off far too quickly. They then effectively cut each other's throats, and allow a horse that has been ridden off the pace to come through and win.

Many races are run at what we would call even pace – neither too fast, nor too slow, and with horses able to challenge from anywhere. So, we won't be worrying about pace as a factor for all races.

What we want to identify is if a race is likely to be run in one of the above more extreme patterns. The details covering each horses' last few runs includes comments on how the horse run its race, and these are usually enough for us to guess how the horse may run today. We want to divide the horses into 4 categories:

a)   Committed front runners
b)   Horses that like to race prominently or in the pack
c)   Committed hold up horses
d)   Those we haven't got a clue about.

The comments will enable you to do this fairly easily. Looking at the horses we were examining earlier, Reggie Buck has the following comments for its last five races:
1.   tracked leaders, led 3 out
2.   behind, rapid headway 4th
3.   chased leaders, led approaching 2 out
4.   held up in touch, led approaching 3 out

5.   tracked leaders

I'd put Reggie Buck in Group (b), with a note in my head that he likes to try to attack a few fences from home.

Maximus by contrast has the following comments:
1.   held up in touch
2.   held up
3.   prominent, led 5th
4.   tracked leaders
5.   held up in touch
6.   held up, headway 9th

he has been ridden prominently on occasion, but I think you can comfortably put him in Group C.

Haditovski is more a front-running animal
1.   led to 5th
2.   led after 2nd to 4th
3.   took keen hold, tracked leading pair
4.   always prominent
5.   chased leaders
6.   led until after 1st

He doesn't always lead, but it seems that he's happiest out in front. If he could dominate proceedings he may be very happy indeed.

One thing to be careful about is where the previous races have very few runners (less than 8). Something has to lead a race, and in smaller fields you will often find a reluctant leader. You may find a horse you think is a horse that races prominently or is a hold up horse apart from one race where it led. Check the size of the field in that race – if it's a small field, then it was probably forced to lead.

The 'spotlight' race-reader comments will also often tell you if a horse is a front-runner, and sometimes include comments on the likely pace of the race.

I usually quickly go through the form, scribbling over each horse's form whether it is
L – Front-runner
P – Prominent
H – Hold up
? – Don't know/can't tell

Then look at what you've got. The things I'm most looking for are:

1. Only one front runner. I believe this is still the thing I get most excited about. If there's only one front-runner, and it can dominate at a slowish pace, or nick a healthy lead, it can steal the race. There was a time when this was a system I followed blindly, regardless of the overall chances of the horse concerned. Now I use it as a very positive point about a circled runner.

   You can't say for sure of course. But where I have one front runner and the rest all seem to be committed hold up horses, I can tell you I get pretty excited. This is as true for the jumps as it is for the flat. Unfortunately, often it is so obvious the race-reader points it out as well. This puts it in the public mind, and it will be taken into account in the betting. Where the race-reader hasn't seen it you may well be onto something a bit special. Or completely wrong.

   Where I find one front runner I put a P alongside its circle to show that it is strongly suited to the pace of the race.

2. Lots of front-runners. This is a definite negative for these horses. Here I would put a crossed-out P against any front runners that are circled horses. It is also a plus for hold-up horses. I may put a P against them.

3. No pace. Where you can't find any pace, put a warning by the race title and conditions. The winner can come from

anywhere. Personally, I'd prefer them to be prominent types, but these races tend to be unpredictable. Trainers and jockeys have noticed the lack of a front runner, and often one or more horses not usually associated with front-running will give it a go.

I tend to treat any speed rating with caution in these situations. A horse gets a speed rating from a fast race, not for winning a two furlong sprint. The likely winner may be one that runs well in small fields, where races are often tactical affairs, as opposed to large cavalry-charges, where a true pace is virtually guaranteed.

4. Lots of pace. There may not necessarily be a lot of committed front runners, but there is a decent sized field with the majority of horses preferring to race prominently, or up with the pace. Alternatively, there may be one or two pacemakers in the field to guarantee a true-run race. I do have a preference for hold-up horses in the former type. I would also be interested in horses that have won in big competitive fields before and/or have high speed-ratings. I would give them a P along-side their circle.

I haven't greatly helped you in terms of cast-iron rules. Sorry. If I learn any I'll pass them on. I love analysing the likely pace, and I love backing sole front-runners. Atavus at 40/1 changed one season from the dull to the spectacular. But I've learnt not to overdo it. I've lost count of the times I've framed a race around a likely pace only for a completely different race to unfold.

The Effect of the Draw. (D)

The effect of the draw on flat races can be remarkable. Some trips on some courses are almost entirely reliant on the effect of the draw.

The Racing Post provide details of the likely effect of the draw at each course as part of their course details. These are a fair starting-point but hardly complete. They also study certain races, usually the big sprints, on race day.

There are a number of books written on this subject, and articles appear in the trade press all the time. I do not have enough space here to do credit to this subject, but it is certainly worthy of study.

There are probably as many as 30 draw biases over all manner of trips at certain tracks around the country.

It's something you need to build up a picture of for yourself over time. In some cases, the bias is well known, and the bookies build the bias into the prices. The most obvious ones at the courses we're interested in are:

Chester 5&6 furlongs	Best draw = low: Worst draw = high
Epsom 5 furlongs	Best draw = high
Goodwood 7 furlongs	Best draw = high: Worst draw = low
York 1m 2f	Best draw = low
Sandown 5 furlongs	Best draw = high

When analysing our race, we need to highlight which horses are particularly well-suited by the draw, and which have been handed a near-impossible situation. On the whole I'd be interested in the ones drawn either lowest three or highest three, adjusting slightly for field size – ie going to lowest 5 in a field of, say, 25 runners.

I would put a D alongside each circled horse well-suited by today's draw, and a D crossed-out for a circled horse unsuited. If the draw is particularly likely to affect the race I would make a note at the top of the race stating that the draw will be key, as I did earlier if Pace was going to be a likely key factor.

Pace and Draw (p/d)

The above two factors, pace and draw, sometimes combine together to total more than the sum of their whole. Some courses under certain conditions suit front-runners for example. If you are a front-running horse, you should have an advantage. But that advantage could be accentuated or minimised by the effect of the draw. The front-runner with a draw on the fence maybe in the ideal position to break first and then dictate the pace. The front-runner drawn on the wide outside in a large field will face an almost hopeless task, having to burn up too much energy getting to the front to be able to last home.

And the opposite is also true. The race looks to contain a few front-runners. Your horse is a hold-up horse drawn on the inside rail. The horse is going to need a large slice of luck to get the race to pan out how he desires. A hold-up horse on the wide outside though, can simply drop in behind the runners and make his way into the race slowly.

And so on. Try to get a picture as to how you think the race will be run, and in races where the horses seem particularly well or badly suited by the combination of pace and draw write 'pd' or 'pd' crossed-out alongside the circled runner.

Racing Post figures *(Circle Postmark figure)*

In circling our horses, we haven't acknowledged that some of them may have stronger claims than others on the bare form. We have effectively given them all an even chance. I used to have a star system so that strong form horses stood out from weak ones. I abandoned this over time as it wasn't helping me. Instead I have included some 'form' based ratings as part of my alternative handicapping. If a horse is well clear on form, it will stand out because a number of 'alternative' factors will highlight its ability.

Three of these form part of the race-card.

(a)   Each horse receives a number, printed next to a picture of the silks the jockey will be wearing, which is the Racing Post's *'Postmark'*, or private handicapping mark, adjusted to take into account today's weight. The highest number relates to the top-rated horse, and this number is highlighted by the paper as being the top mark.

(b)   Underneath the Spotlight comments there are two recommendations. The first of these is the *Postdata* selection. *Postdata* is an attempt by the Racing Post to do something very similar to what we've been doing so far, examine basic form factors to come up with the horse most likely to win the race.

(c)   The other selection is the *Topspeed* selection, for the horse the racing Post believes will be the fastest, based on their speed figures.

If all three factors recommend the same horse, (and it is a circled horse), I circle the Postform figure and put a figure 3 by it. It suggests that the horse in question really does have a lot going for it today.

If the Postform and Topspeed figures point to the same horse, (and it is a circled horse) I circle the Postform figure and put a figure 2 by it. This is still worthy of note. In all other cases I ignore the ratings.

Weekender Topspeed rating (TS)

Not only do I take notice of the Racing Post speed figure, but I also like to see who is the top-rated in the Weekender. Perhaps surprisingly the speed ratings are different even though they are sister papers. This is because the Weekender used to belong to the Sporting Life. The Life's speed guru, Dave Edwards seems to have survived the merger, probably because his ratings are exceptional. The Weekender is on sale on Wednesday, which means it prints speed ratings for all entries for the weekend. Come Saturday half of the entries will have pulled out. That means you'll have to take a few seconds to work out which is the highest rated horse actually running. Once you have identified it, write TS next to that horse's name in the Racing Post, ONLY if it is a circled horse.

Your own Speed Ratings (The actual speed numbers)

At the risk of making you think I'm obsessed by speed, I also compile my own speed ratings for the top horses. I do this using the Weekender and a system detailed by Nick Mordin in his book, Betting for a Living. He has also written a book exclusively on speed – Mordin on Time. I recommend either for anyone who also wants to compile speed ratings.

I don't compile mine in quite the same way as Nick, nor do I follow them in the same way. What I attempt to do is to identify horses that are very fast indeed, and so capable of winning top races.

I only keep a record of a speed figure if it is a very high one which in my system means over 80. If a horse has a rating of 90 or over that tends to suggest it can win a Grade 1 race.

A horse with more than one speed rating over 80 in a season has also proven itself to be tough and competitive at the highest level, in races with genuine pace. Limiting my study to fast races means I only have to do ratings for the big meetings, and so I only spend half an hour each week compiling figures and updating my figures.

I keep a basic spreadsheet for each season listing the qualifying horses in alphabetical order, with their rating alongside, along with when and where the rating was achieved. I will usually end the season with a couple of hundred listings. Where a circled horse has previously gained a rating, I write the rating or ratings down alongside the horse's name in the Racing Post. These ratings are really useful at the big end of season National Hunt festivals – Cheltenham and Aintree.

Private Handicap Ratings from Clive Weight (CW)

A final rating system I use is the private form-ratings compiled by Clive Weight for the top races in the Weekender. These appear alongside the entries in the Weekender. I always make a note of the top-rated horse running in each race. If it is one of my circled horses I write CW alongside its name in the Racing Post. Clive Weight is a very shrewd judge, and his ratings are good money-spinners for him. Unfortunately, they usually highlight the favourite, but can be a good indicator of a solid favourite.

Training Centre comments *(TC)*

I have very little time for supposed privileged information straight from the horse's mouth. I'd feel differently I'm sure if I had my own mole in a major training yard. The closest I come to anything like that is looking at the reports from each Training Centre found at the back of the Weekender. It's fair to say these vary in quality, but I like to make a note of the naps of each Centre, and note the horse with a TC if it is a circled horse.

I am also quite intrigued if they tip up a 'circled' horse that is likely to be a long price. I don't know that for sure yet, as we haven't even looked at the prices. For some races though I will have a good idea of the likely favourites without looking at the prices, as I will know the horses involved, and will already have a pattern forming from the work I have already done. If one catches my eye I make a note of it again.

Trends *(trends)*

Major races are often won year after year by similar types of horses. There are two places to find this information. *Codebreaker* in the Weekender analyses the major race of the weekend, and comes up with one tip. Trends are also studied in the Racing Post, usually covering most of the major races. If both Codebreaker and the Racing Post Trends tip up the same horse and it is circled I certainly make a note of it by writing *trends* alongside the horse in question. They don't usually come up with the same horse, and when they do it is worthy of note.

The reason they don't tend to tip the same horse is that both articles tend to have to filter the horses through sufficient factors to find one horse. This means that the real key information is lost in the face of more spurious eliminators. I'm more interested in seeing if there are one or two major trends in the race. Often races are framed so that they suit a particular weight range, or age of horse.

For instance, the last 12 winners of the Welsh National have all previously won at Chepstow, and 9 out of 10 winners ran at Chepstow's early December meeting. These are remarkable trends worth noting.

As another example the Hennessey Gold Cup has gone to a second season chaser 9 times in the last 13 years, and to horses proven over 3 miles or further. I will make suitable notes, small crosses and ticks, say, that mean something to me – for example a tick alongside all second season jumpers who have won over 3m+

Jockeys *(Circle jockey's name)*

My Aunt Lil was one for the jockey. Aren't we all? Look at the effect Frankie's 7-timer had on the bookies.

Aunt Lil may have been where I got my love of horses from. She was a tough old bird. She was a conductress on the 37 bus from Peckham to Hounslow and back through the war years; married a jail-bird who died young; re-invented herself as a nanny to a long-forgotten soul group in Beverly Hills (The Fifth Generation), where her adventures included unarming and arresting a house-breaker; before retiring to Benidorm, with Sky TV and a bottle of gin a day for company. Her winner-finding strategy consisted of looking closely at what Willie Carson and Pat Eddery were riding, and choosing one of them. When challenged on the wisdom of this, she'd take a drag on her fag and a swig of her gin, and say – "well, top jockeys, they don't ride rubbish, they don't."

I've been to both extremes with jockeys. I spent some time in the early days blindly following my favourite jockeys. And I spent a lot of time paying them no consideration whatsoever, which I've come to the conclusion is also not recommended.

A few points worth bearing in mind.

Flat jockeys

Flat jockeys are small. Incredibly small. Stop and stare small. Sorry, but that's how it is. Now, it's fairly unusual to be stop and stare small. In fact, I've only met a couple of people like that who aren't actually jockeys (one of them being my Gran who measures a remarkable 4 ft 9 inches in her slippers). I'm sure it's an incredibly competitive area of work, but it's not quite like football is it. At least with football you know that the top professionals have proven themselves more able than millions of other hopefuls.

Which leaves me to believe that whilst sadly a lot of flat jockeys may have to starve themselves; work ridiculously long hours; suck-up to a bunch of obnoxious owners; and drive thousands of miles for a chance of a spare ride, none of this means they're actually any good. Quite a few of them seem barely able to point their horse in the right direction and let it run. Rarely do they seem to have studied the race, thought about the likely pace, or the effect of the draw, or walked the course, and so on.

Their major talent seems to be in running their horses up the back-side of the eventual winner, weaving off a straight-line in a driving finish, and dropping their hands in the shadow of the post, costing you that life-changing combination forecast.

Which gives some advantage to those jockeys who are obviously highly skilled. It's probably best to have a list of jockeys who you believe have an edge, I've supplied my own lists below.

Jump jockeys

Jump jockeys are completely mad. Barking. If you don't believe me go and stand by the railway fences at Sandown. These idiots will ride any old nag over these fences – for fun. After all it's not like most of them make a semblance of a living out of the sport. And then when they have broken half the bones in their body after some calamity involving three-legged Novice chasers, they'll rush themselves back into the saddle quicker than Darren Anderton can recover from cutting his toe-nails. Now, as with very small people, I haven't met too many people in normal life who are completely barking, so I guess the same rules must apply to jump jockeys as it does to flat ones.

Some further pointers.

One problem is that the best jockeys are usually the ones getting the best rides, and are the ones the public are over-betting. I can't have AP McCoy on my own list simply because any horse he rides will be too short, owing to all those who back him blind. Indeed, the top 6 jump jockeys have such a good agent now that they are able to hoover up virtually all the good spare rides, thus perpetuating the notion that they are the best 6 jockeys.

At the other end of the scale I certainly wouldn't put you off having a list of jockeys to avoid. In fact, I'd recommend it strongly. Having criticised jockeys generally, I'm certainly not going to compound that by singling some of them out for extra bile. Suffice to say I know who they are, and if you keep your eyes peeled so will you,

Obviously, there's no point reading any significance into riding arrangements if the jockey on board is the retained rider for the stable. Particularly, a small stable. He isn't riding the horse because the owner's paid him a gazillion quid. He's riding the horse because he gets up half an hour before he went to bed to ride out the entire stable string; to school a couple of uncoordinated juveniles; to muck out some flatulent old rogue; and to drive the horse-box 200 miles to some gaff track for one ride under strict orders to lose at all costs.

I am however interested in jockeys riding outside their yard. If they're on my plus list and they're riding a circled horse, I'm inclined to circle their name. Sadly, if they've made it onto my 'avoid' list, and they are riding a circled horse I put a cross through their name.

You can also use statistics to back up your opinions. The Racing Post has jockey statistics, and these will provide total statistics, and figures for the jockey when riding for their main stable. Some basic maths will tell you how well they do on all their other rides. I suggest you look here as a means of starting your own lists.

I'm also interested in jockeys with remarkable strike rates with certain trainers, and this table will provide details of that as well, as will the jockey table for each course.

Sometimes jockey arrangements just jump out the page at you. Here's just a few:
(a) A top jockey (eg McCoy) granted permission not to ride one of his stable's (Pipe's) horses in favour of another stable's fancied runner.
(b) A top jockey, over from Ireland or France, picking up a spare ride on a relatively unfancied (but circled) horse, for an unfashionable stable.
(c) Jockeys travelling a fair way to fit in two meetings in one day, with only one ride at one of the tracks.
(d) A jockey stopping just short of disembowelment to get to a weight way below their normal weight for one key ride – (eg McCoy getting down to 10 stone).

These sorts of pointers could make me put a circle around the jockey's name if the horse he's riding is circled.

My own rather select 'A' Lists of jockeys who I love to see on my horses:

Flat	Jumps
Frankie Dettori (outside rides)	Mick Fitzgerald
Mick Kinane (outside rides)	Jimmy McCarthy (front runners)
Olivier Peslier	Richard Guest
Richard Hughes	Ruby Walsh
Darryll Holland	Paul Flynn
Jimmy Fortune (front runners)	Tony Dobbin (down south)
Pat Eddery (sprints)	Norman Williamson
Jamie Spencer	

Other patterns *(various)*

There are plenty of other handicapping factors that can be taken into account. Nick Mordin's book covers quite a few. One example would be his notion of what he calls a 'rest pattern'. This suggests that some horses need a good break between their races, (over 40 days) but when they do get a break go particularly well fresh.

Handicapping factors such as these, are becoming common currency these days. I am always interested in them and, although I don't actively seek them out, if they are mentioned somewhere in the notes, or I happen to know them about a certain horse, I will mark them up next to a circled runner.

One book, titled *Profile,* which is published each season for flat and for jumps racing focuses on highlighting patterns in a horse's performance. It outlines going, distance, and course preferences as well as preferences for field size, left hand or right hand tracks, flat or undulating, galloping or sharp tracks and so on. I have bought it a few times, and recommend it. I haven't really found a way to benefit fully from it myself.

One notable pattern is the inability of top-weights to win the top handicap races, over a distance. I can hardly think of an example of a winning horse. This is usually reflected in the prices. However, quite a few run placed, and can make cracking each way bets. They are also great pointers for championship races – and I always note an eye-catching run off top-weight, for example Lord Noelie in the 2001 Hennessey Gold Cup.

Tipsters

I don't see the point of following tipsters. Given that the major attraction to racing for me is being proven right, it's anathema to me to abdicate responsibility for a selection to someone else.

However, I do find myself taking more notice of some people than I do of others, and I like to take account of this within this alternative handicapping process. In terms of tipsters I take a keen interest in the following:

1. **Gerald Delamere.** *(GD)*
   Gerald is a tipster who writes for both the Weekender and the racing Post on major racing days. In the Weekender he reviews the week's racing in the South, highlighting horses that could go on to win again, and highlighting likely losers as well. He's very astute at identifying possible future races that would suit horses, and fairly open at pointing out horses that weren't trying their hardest to win. Each week he produces a list of horses to follow. I have no idea if these are profitable or not (probably not or else the Weekender would have advertised the fact of his success), but I wouldn't put anybody off using such a list as a further means of alternative handicapping.

For our purposes, I prefer his Saturday column. Here he takes the big races and analyses the strengths of the runners. I will always put 'GD' alongside his selection, if circled, and often a '(GD)' around his second choice. His second choice is often a good-priced outsider, and given our ultimate search is for value, I've found this can often be a significant pointer.

2. *Pricewise* (PW)

A few people have come and gone running the Pricewise column in the Post. The column aims to identify 'value' bets. However, during good spells when the Post promotes it quite heavily it can have a startling affect on the market. As it has a similar approach to what we're trying to do, we have to take an interest in its findings.

I've lost count of the times when I've started to get excited analysing a race because it's become obvious that a likely long-shot has a huge amount going for him, only to turn to Pricewise and find that he's napped the horse in big bold letters, and that the 33/1 has long since gone, replaced by 12/1 in a place.

Any horse that Pricewise has tipped, that is circled, I put a 'PW' alongside the horse's name.

3. *Nick Mordin* (NM)

It must be obvious by now how much Nick has influenced me. He writes in the Weekender, and I make a note of anything he says. He often comes up with fascinating systems, that he believes will show a profit, at least until too many people catch onto them. I've followed many of them with success. If I'm following any I will make a note along-side a circled horse that it is a system contender.

He also has a tipping line. My advice re tipping lines is save your money. They usually charge an obscene rate per minute to listen to a truck-full of waffle about yesterday's unlucky losers, before tipping up hundreds of odds-on certainties in ambiguous phrases – 'sure to be there or thereabouts' – so that they can be selective about which ones they actually tipped once the results are known.

However, I do tend to have a listen to Nick's line. Especially on a big racing day, or when there is top French or American racing. He always gives the tips within the first minute. If his tips are 'circled horses', I write 'NM' along-side their name.

4. ***First Show.*** (FS)
Malcom Heyhoe pens this article for the Weekender. It aims to get people on a horse that's value on the Wednesday before the weekend's big race, or sometimes ante post for the major races of the year. I do occasionally throw a few quid onto a horse on the Wednesday, as a result of his analysis, which is hardly in the spirit of this book. The problem is his article does affect the prices, and so you have to take a view. Whether the prices have gone or not come the Saturday, his reading of the race is always interesting.

5. ***Ladbrokes prices.*** (Lads)
Quite a few people make a note of this. John McCririck often says this in his immediate post-race analysis. 'Ladbrokes (or another bookies) knew. They only went 10s when everyone else went 14s in the morning prices.'.

The point is that the odds compilers are highly competent. The market they form is very close (and contrived). When a big company goes off on a limb about a horse it's worth noting. I'm always interested when a bookie is generously out of line, and if I see one going double the odds of the price generally offered I certainly sit up and take notice. Unfortunately, the price is usually long-gone before I can take advantage of it – it's the one time where I'm tempted to bet without any of this 'form' study.

However, it's also of interest when Ladbrokes (or Hills) goes short on a horse compared to the rest. Bookmakers have stable intelligence that would shame MI5, and if they feel so strongly about a horse that they don't want to touch it at any price, I feel I have to take note of that. You will also get a feel as to which bookies are particularly close to which stables. Ladbrokes seems very sensitive as to the fortunes of the O'Brien empire. The odds they are offering compared to other bookies can be very useful when O'Brien runs 2 or 3 runners in the one race,

Where a horse is eye-catchingly shorter with Ladbrokes than with other bookmakers, and the horse is a circled horse, I write 'LADS' alongside the horse's name.

That's as many 'alternative handicapping' factors as I use at the moment. I am always looking for new ideas, trying out new factors and systems, and so the list changes with time.

Below are some brief notes on other factors that could be used.

Private handicap Ratings
You could always compile your own handicap ratings, as I do with my speed ratings. There are books that can show you how to do this, but I'd suggest it's pretty much common sense.

I am currently concentrating on the better Novice Chases. These suit me very well as there are only a few a week, and you can see most of them on TV. They are also run off level weights (plus penalties) making it easier to give a rating. It's an attempt on my part to gain a feel for collateral form.

It has provided one bet so far, that of opposing Barton with Le Cabro D'or. Barton was long odds on, based on his hurdling form, but had been far from fluent in his first race over fences. Le Cabro D'or had jumped well from the front in his first race, beating a decent horse that had won well next time out. They seemed very close to me on chance, and my form ratings gave Le Cabro D'Or the edge. Le Cabro D'or was 3/1, and became a major bet for me. He lost, by miles in the end, but Barton jumped sloppily enough for me to feel pleased with the wager.

Breeding

I've always been interested in sires' performance as a predictor of a horse's preferences. Two things I'm very interested in are:

1. Whether a top 3 year old is going to get a mile and a half. There seem to be less and less horses these days that are bred to get a distance. If you can find the ones bred to stay, or better still bred not to stay, you should be able to winkle out some nice bets.

2. A horse's preference for extremes of going. Whilst I've said this is an over-rated factor, obviously, some horses are very much affected by the going. You can see by some horse's exaggerated knee action that they are going to be happier in the mud, whilst some horses seem to float over firm ground. Breeding looks to be a good guide to this.

There are books that look at the effect of breeding. There was a great book at one stage called 'Bred' by Tim Coe that came out each flat season, which created a bit of a stir for a while. He was very useful for looking at 2 year old races and maiden races. As these became areas I pretty much avoided I stopped paying much attention to him. I think he disappeared onto the internet as a paid for tipping service, and so fell off my radar screen.

Weekender Notebook
In their results service in the Weekender, there are attached notes about horses the race-readers feel are likely to win pretty soon. These may be worth following of highlighting against circled horses' names.

Mark Your Card
This is a similar service to the Weekender notebook, but the Racing Post version. On each race-day they have a column highlighting which horses have been noted in the mark your card feature.

7 day runners
Horses re-appearing within 7 days of winning their last outing are considered noteworthy animals. Indeed, Braddock gives a few pages to them in his book, believing they are the best type of animal to bet on. He quotes figures for the 1988-89 season where 32.2% of hurdle and 33.3% of chase winners who raced again within a 7 day period won. Similar figures are provided for flat racing. Startling figures.

One side element of this I like is if a horse races twice at the same festival. This tends to mean the horse is at the top of its game, and is a tough old character. They have provided some nice bets, especially each way at the Cheltenham and Aintree festivals over the years.

The Racing Post has a column detailing horses reappearing within 7 days.

Gallops reports

The weekender carries gallops reports from the main training centres. These include comments noting if a major jockey is riding out a particular horse, or if one horse went much better than the others it was training with. I have never used this, but I can see how it could be used as a modifier.

Weekender entries

Again, this is something I've played with from time to time, without finding a real angle. The Weekender lists all horses due to be engaged over the weekend in alphabetical order, detailing the races each is declared for. It also carries cards for each of the meetings, race by race. Two things should be interesting:

a)   Where a horse is engaged in more than one race. It's fascinating to look at the options for a horse, and try to think why the trainer chose this option. I am most interested in looking at a horse when the trainer has chosen a really hard option, when the horse was also engaged in a much easier race. I take this as a vote of confidence more often than not.

b)   Where a trainer has declared a lot of runners for the race. I usually think they fancy farming this race and so pay attention to their final selection. They usually are big yards and have good collateral form lines for the other runners, meaning they may have a good idea as to the chances of the one they finally leave in.

Ratings – Improver.

The Racing Post carries a table looking at past ratings of horses engaged in handicaps. For a while in jump races I followed this whereby I noted any horse whose rating was either the same or higher each successive race. This seemed to me to be conclusive proof that the horse was an improver, and so likely to improve today. It worked well in National Hunt, but that was in the days when the handicapper put horses up in weight relatively slowly, compared to today.

The alternative' ideas are only limited by your imagination or the time it may take to see if they add any value to your process.

The key rule for me is that they are all modifiers, rather than stand alone winner finders. Many, including Nick Mordin, talk about the need to find an edge. They say that you need to find a factor still under-considered by the betting public and betting using this factor will guarantee value and an edge, at least until the public cotton on to it.

I have tried this in the past. But for me, any of these factors need to be integrated into an overall study of the race. I've grown away from betting on the strength of just one factor.

You should now have the race-card, with each short-listed race and a number supplementary scribbles all over it.

Chapter 4 – Pricing the race

'Come on, Man Utd must have a great chance now – must be some value there' 'Yes, but what chance exactly?'
(A conversation between gambling syndicate members)

In this chapter, we'll work through a few examples to show you how to price a race. Let's start with some fairly easy examples in the world of sport, where you'll probably be able to take a view without having to do any form study or investigating.

The Ryder Cup never actually took place in 2001, but that doesn't stop us pricing it up. There are only three possible results – a win for either US or Europe, or a tie. To make a book all you need to do is divide 100% across the three results depending on how likely you think it is for each event to happen.

Write down what you think the proportions are next to each outcome below BEFORE turning the page.

Outcome	your % chance
US win	
Europe win	
Match tied	
	_____
Total	100

Now turn over the page and see both how I priced it up, and how the bookies priced it up.

Outcome	My%	Bookies%
US win	55	64
Europe win	33	33
Match tied	12	9
Total percent	100	106

Compare your spread, with both mine and with the bookies. The first thing to notice about the bookies is their numbers total 106, rather than 100. This is the bookies' margin, or what is called the over-round. Basically, the bookies offer under-the-odds on each eventuality. That will mean, as long as they make a fair spread of bets, they will make a small profit whatever happens. In this instance their odds compilers will have done the same as me and spread 100% across the three options, coming up with something like 62% chance of a US win, 31% of a European and 7% chance of a tie. They then added 2% to each option to get the numbers above, and so build in their profit margin.

2% per possible outcome is a good rule of thumb for working out what the bookies margin is likely to be. Many of the big handicaps have spreads equating to 145% or more. Don't even think about golf tournaments.
They don't put the 2% on evenly, that was just my way of explaining it. Often the favourite is much shorter odds than the bookies think they should be.

Say the bookies were offering odds on two even money chances – classically a coin coming down head or tails. Obviously, they wouldn't go evens, they'd go 10/11 or similar on both. If the betting public bet evenly they'll be able to guarantee a profit whatever the outcome. Perfection for bookies. But what if the public, spurred on by a couple of tipsters who believe *Heads* is a good thing, decide they only want to back *Heads*. Now the bookies are going to have to adjust the prices big-time. They could end up going 1/2 on *Heads* and 7/4 *Tails* in an attempt to stop people backing Heads, and to get some money for tails.

Anyway, back to learning about how percentage chances translate into odds.
The starting-point is that 50% is equivalent to Evens.

Overleaf is a table that looks at all likely odds and what percentage they relate to. This will become a really important tool when we look at later tables.

You should be able to say roughly what each price compares to in percentage terms. I'd concentrate on getting to grips with it in a basic way, concentrating on some key figures and using whole numbers as a guide.

The key figures for me are:

Evens	50%
2/1	33%
3/1	25%
4/1	20%
5/1	17%
6/1	14%
8/1	11%
10/1	9%
14/1	7%
20/1	5%

For 'odds on' percentages, take the odds against percentage and subtract it from 100. So, 2/1 on is equal to 100 – 2/1 against = 66%. 1/8 is equal to 100 minus 8/1 = 89% and so on.

In the Ryder Cup the odds I came up with, and the ones the bookies came up with were as follows.

Outcome	My%	My Odds	Bookie%	Bookie Odds
US win	55	4/5	64	4/7
Europe win	33	2/1	33	2/1
Match tied	12	15/2	9	10/1

We'll leave aside any idea as to value until the next chapter. Suffice to say, the bookies' odds on either side winning are shorter than my own. However, they are offering longer odds than my own on the match being tied.

Let's take another sports event, this time on the outright winner of the 2002 World Cup, looking at prices at Xmas 2001, after the draw was made.

And let's introduce the idea of making a book only concentrating on the 'circled' runners. My 'circled' runners for the World Cup, consisting of the only teams I can actually envisage winning the tournament would be the eight favourites comprising all the major football nations.

I'm not going to price up all the other teams as they don't interest me as betting propositions. All I need to do is come up with a total proportionate chance of there being an almighty upset and one of those teams actually winning. I decide on that representing a 10% chance.

The rest of my book needs to add up to 90%.

The 8 teams I need to allocate 90% across are Argentina, France, Brazil, Italy, England, Germany, Spain and Portugal. It seems to me that France and Argentina are the best two teams in the world and the most likely winners. France have the easier draw, but for me may be a team in slight decline, whereas Argentina may be reaching their peak. I'm going to let these two factors balance each other out and allocate the two nations the same chance as each other. The two teams I've only included on past reputation are Germany and Brazil. I don't think either of them will win, but I can't bring myself to cross them out. Brazil also have a ridiculously easy draw which we have to take into account.

Italy and Portugal are my idea of the two strongest European teams outside France and have good draws. England, (and Germany) I worry about because of the weather. England also has a terrible draw and, like Spain, perennially under-achieve.

If I was to put them into 3 pots, I'd have France and Argentina in the top set, Germany, England, Spain and Brazil in the unlikely set, and Portugal and Italy in the middle set. And I'd allocate proportions across those groups of

Group 1 – Argentina and France   40%
Group 2 – Portugal and Italy   20%
Group 3 - Germany, Brazil, England, Spain   30%
Then, looking at each pot and divvying up my percentages accordingly, I'd end up with a book as follows:

Team	My %	My odds	General bookie odds
Argentina	20%	4/1	4/1
France	20%	4/1	4/1
Italy	11%	8/1	6/1
Portugal	9%	10/1	11/1
Brazil	8%	12/1	13/2
England	8%	12/1	12/1
Spain	8%	12/1	10/1
Germany	6%	14/1	14/1

The first thing to add is that I go 10% the field. The bookies price up the rest of the field at odds between 33/1 and 200/1, totalling 30% of the book. They are betting 100% on the first 8 teams and thus 130% in total.

It's encouraging to me that my odds are quite close to the bookies. If I was way out of line I would need to question whether I had sufficient reason.

If I was to price up my odds for real I would be knocked over in the rush for the Brazil price, and would soon have to cut it. That's the one price that's well out of line. However, I don't have to offer odds and that allows me to have whatever outrageous odds in my book I feel I can justify. And I do feel this represents Brazil's chances more accurately than the prices offered. That's what I love about betting, needing to have strong opinions against the normal flow.

So, I'm happy with my book. That's all we need to worry about for now. In the following chapters, we'll come back to this and look at how to determine value, and what possible bets there may be.

Let's now look at a couple of horse races. For the first one let's look at the horse race we used originally.

The first thing to do is decide what proportion of the 100% you are going to allocate to the 6 horses you have decided can't win. This is a true art and will depend on many things. We will spend quite a lot of time on this in later chapters on 'value', on using a bank and on psychological aspects, so this is a basic starting-point.

Here is a very simple approach.

Each circled horse will be given one point and each uncircled horse will be given one third of a point. The total is divided into 100% and then multiplied by the number of circled horses.

In this example. There are 11 runners. 5 are 'circled' and 6 are uncircled. Each circled horse gets 1 point = 5 points. Each uncircled horse gets one third of a point – 6 x 1/3 = 2 points. The total points are 7. 100 divided by 7 = 14.3%. 5 circled horses multiplied by 14.3% = 71.5%. Therefore, in this race you allocate 71.5% to the 5 circled horses and 28.5% to the 6 uncircled horses.

I would tend to round down and say 70% is available to the circled horses.
The bigger the field the more you'd move the numbers down, in big fields I'd be going half points per each uncircled horse. Where you have circled most of the field though, you could go lower, to a quarter point.

So, for this race we could have 70% available for the circled runners. As it happens, I decided to price the race fairly cautiously for reasons we'll look at later and I went 66% or two thirds likelihood that the horses I had circled would win the race in question.

What we need to do is open our large notebook, and write down the details of the race

C Class Showcase handicap hurdle – Newbury – good going, 2 miles. 11 run. 5 'circled' horses. Book = 66%

Then write down the names of the runners in early price order, stopping at the last horse you have circled. Leave a space to the left-hand side. On this left-hand side, we need to make a note of all the alternative handicapping factors we found for each horse and marked on the race-card in the Racing Post.

We need to put a line through the uncircled horses, and also write a note of the general bookie price alongside each horse.

Our page would look as follows:

PW	Batswing	11/4
	Victory Roll	5/1
TF/lads	Haditovski	11/2
	~~Reggie Buck~~	6/1
TRC	~~Carandrew~~	13/2
	~~Iris Collonges~~	7/1
J	Marble Arch	12/1
	Maximus	14/1

We have 66 points to allocate across our 5 runners. Again, this is an art not a science. We seem to be left with three favourites and two outsiders, so we should split the points across the groups accordingly. I'm going to give the three favourites a 50% chance of winning the race between them, leaving 16% for the two outsiders.

I split the points as follows, including translating into odds, as it would look in your book

PW	Batswing	11/4	20%	4/1
	Victory Roll	5/1	14%	6/1
TF/lads	Haditovski	11/2	18%	9/2
	~~Reggie Buck~~	6/1		
TRC	~~Carandrew~~	13/2		
	~~Iris Collonges~~	7/1		
J	Marble Arch	12/1	10%	9/1
	Maximus	14/1	6%	14/1

I've ended up with 68 points, halfway between the 66 and 70 points, something I'm happy with. I did it in pencil and fiddled around with the figures until I was happy with them. The key guide is the alternative handicapping factors on the left –hand side. They represent your potential edge. The bookies' odds represent your reality check. The bookies' over-round represents a suitable margin of error.

Haditovski has a couple of nice pointers to it, a trainer in form and Ladbrokes being short on the horse, whereas Victory Roll has nothing going for it other than its obvious form chance. I nearly didn't even circle Victory Roll and so I'm going to be happy to go long on it. Batswing is tipped by Pricewise, but has no other handicapping pointers. Of the three, Batswing looks the favourite, but I place Haditovski close to it with Victory Roll just behind. Of the two outsiders, I am very much taken with the fact that this is Ruby Walsh's only ride of the day on Marble Arch, whereas Maximus only has the form chance. I'm happy to split the 16% generously in Marble Arch's favour.

I'm taking a big chance on this race on the three in the middle that I have crossed out. The bookies go 40% those three, whereas I give them plus the other three outsiders only 32% between them. That shows the importance of the first part of the book, circling the right horses. I am still happy to work to those odds, being fairly confident I have identified clear reasons why those three will not be winning.

I'm happy with my book.

Chapter 5 – Finding Value

"And the rest of the world think we are all total nutters, but they can go and talk to their back-sides for all I care. Because they are all just fruit-loops who don't know what it is to believe in something which is hard to see, or to keep looking for something which is totally hard to find."
('Pobby and Dingan' - Ben Rice)

So, let's review what we've done so far.

1. We decided what races to concentrate on.
2. We studied each of these races and came up with a list of 'circled' horses which we believe have a chance of winning
3. We looked at alternative handicapping methods and made notes against each circled horse accordingly.
4. We wrote down the details of the race in our notebook, listing all the horses in odds order, down to the last circled horse, and made a book, including an overall percentage for the uncircled horses (the field)

It's 10:30 and we're nowhere near making a bet. What we need to do now is have a look at what we've got and have a look at the odds on offer, and see where the value may lie in each race.

Value is a tricky concept. It's certainly one my wife doesn't understand when I say about a losing bet – 'Ah, yes but what cracking value.' 'Where's the value in a loser?' she'll reply leaving me unsure whether she means the bet or the bettor.

It's also a highly subjective and hugely arrogant subject. In fact, if you're not prepared to have an opinion you may not be ideally suited to this approach to gambling.

Effectively the concept of value relies on two things. Firstly, the belief that you can price a race up more accurately than the bookies. And secondly, that your opinion will be more accurate than the bulk of punters who will be affecting the prices by their own choices.

Let's go back to the Ryder Cup prices as an easy starting place.

Outcome	My Odds	Bookie Odds
US win	4/5	4/7
Europe win	2/1	2/1
Match tied	15/2	10/1

Hindsight is a wonderful thing. But this is a perfect example because we will never know who was right, so we won't be able to re-run that conversation between my wife and I.

When I price up the race I am already blessed with a built-in margin of error. This margin is the bookie's over-round. Remember that I priced my odds up based on 100% probability – the bookie priced it up to 106%. The bookie built in a small profit margin.

What it means is I should really expect not to come up with any price that is shorter than the bookmakers. This is often the case, especially in large fields where there's a massive profit margin built-in.

I am also blessed that I don't have to offer the odds on every horse, so I don't have to take into account in my prices the general betting public. This is crucial.

Remember the bookie really wants to balance his books so that whatever wins he can make a profit. Unfortunately, this rarely happens because he can't get the public to place a sufficient spread of bets to allow that to happen. So each bookie will also be adjusting their odds, based on the two criteria above – their own hunches and information about the probable winners and losers, and their anticipation as to the likely weight of money for each runner.

My prices can take a less cluttered view.

Favourites and Outsiders.

Favourites

Favourites are nearly always priced much shorter than they should be. The general betting public likes to bet favourites. They like to put them together in combination bets. They like a 'sure thing'. They like the feeling of picking the winners of races and want to repeat that buzz, to feel they are being successful even if it means they are losing in the long-run. A win is like that fruit machine moment when all the lights flash and loads of coins thud into the winnings tray, and people look over at you, and you feel like you've hit the big time with your line of oranges, even though it only pays out £4 and you've just put in £5.

Favourites are like that. Some horses demand to be favourite whatever their real chances, given today's conditions. Here's just a few examples.

a) They're a famous horse with a big following (Florida Pearl)
b) They're from a stable that excels in this race, or at this course
c) It's a talking horse - one the media has latched onto as a potential wonder horse
d) It's a talented horse moving from one discipline to another – eg flat to hurdles, or hurdles to fences against horses it used to beat in the old discipline
e) Lots of tipping lines have jumped on this horse.

f)   It's the last leg of a potential 7 timer for Frankie Dettorri and the whole nation is backing it, and the betting-shops have huge liabilities.

The last one is a great example. Frankie's Ascot 7 timer is a salutary lesson on the betting habits of the nation. There is little doubt in my mind that Frankie rides Ascot better than anyone else. He always has his horse ideally placed as they turn for home. But the day he rode 7 winners wasn't any old racing day. It was a day of great quality. Tough competitive racing. And yet prior to this no-one had gone through the card, even at lowly tracks. God knows how many times Pipe and McCoy have failed to do so with 6 odds-on shots at lowly Taunton or Exeter.

Prior to racing Frankie would have been delighted to have one winner. And so should anyone who followed Frankie. The public backing Frankie blind, in Yankees and accumulators was just madness – and a source of untold riches for bookies over the years.

This was the one day when the tables were turned. Yet that money will have been given back and much more besides on people doing the same and even more so, ever since that fateful day.

In the morning, on the 7th race, the horse Frankie was riding was priced at 12/1. Little indication that it was a likely winner. I remember it well because out of all of Frankie's rides it was actually the only one I was interested in. I had determined that it had roughly a 12% chance and so should be 7/1. It was a potential value bet.

As Frankie started winning two things happened. Firstly, the weight of money running on in doubles etc was causing the bookies to have horrifically one-sided books. They couldn't take enough money on the other runners to balance all the money running onto Frankie's horses. Also, punters around the country who were backing in singles were starting to jump onto the bandwagon, playing up their winnings, or generally getting caught up in the excitement of it all. The bookies had to cut and cut the odds of Frankie's runners to odds that bore no relation to their 'true' odds.

The 7th race horse did not start at 12/1. It didn't even start around the 7/1 I had it down for. It started a 3/1 favourite, a horse with little worthwhile form, and definitely no 25% chance of winning.

And it won. Blimey – that's sport for you. But it sure as hell wasn't value.

To a much lesser extent that's exactly what happens at every race meeting. They have rhythms all of their own that determine how the betting public bet and how bookies lay prices.

And that's something we can take advantage of.

Outsiders

Outsiders are another example. People like the unexpected. There's even people willing to back Elvis still being alive at something like 250/1. Strange results can and do happen. But not often. Bookmakers have to price up all eventualities. And the long-shots are invariably priced shorter than they should be. We like long odds – we're seduced by them. Even when it's a really stingy price, 100/1 still seems a massive price. It can win us a fortune. We forget that the real likelihood of say China winning the World Cup isn't 150/1 but 20,000/1 or more.

The World Cup book that the bookies offer allocates 30% to the outsider nations, whereas I allocated just 10% to them. The bookies don't care. They know that there'll be plenty of Slovenians and Tunisians etc having small patriotic bets at ridiculously short prices, just for the hell of it.

Delicate mechanism

And weight of money will matter to the mid-range of odds as well. Let's return to our World Cup betting.

I priced Brazil at a 12/1, and the bookies were generally offering 13/2. I may well be completely wrong. Their chance may be much more than the 8% I'm working on. That's a stand I have to make, but to my mind that's their true odds.

What I do know is that if I had to take bets on the World Cup, and had to take bets on all the teams, I wouldn't be pricing Brazil up at 12/1. And there are two reasons for that. Firstly, I know I am going against the crowd. Regardless of the fact that Brazil are really struggling at the moment, when it comes to backing the winner of the World Cup many people will want to back Brazil.

They're the glamour nation after all. Plenty of people will be buying the shirts, adopting them for the tournament, (especially after our own ignominious exit). It's accepted wisdom that they are the best football nation on earth. They have won it the most – always back winners. European teams can only win when it's held in Europe, and so on.

If I did go 12/1 I'd be knocked over in the rush. I'd have a completely unbalanced book where everyone came to me for their Brazil bets, and I'd soon have to cut my prices or face bankruptcy.

The second reason is because I wouldn't have to offer such long odds to get takers. The market works as a very delicate mechanism. I only have to be a point or two longer to guarantee takers about a popular team or horse. A lot of people would say – hey look, he's going 8/1 about Brazil, when all the others are going 6/1 or 13/2. So I can guarantee getting as much money as I want by going only slightly longer than the rest of the bookies regardless of my own ideas as to the price it should be. These latter people often confuse getting the best price with getting value. You can still be getting shocking value about the best price.

Having said all of that, the market is a remarkably precise instrument. The long odds-on shots do win more races than the even money shots, and so on. Indeed, one way of measuring your ability to find value will be your ability to beat the declared starting price.

Best Prices

So, the first steps to finding value once you have made your book is to see what the bookies are offering. The second step is to decide if any of their offerings represent value.

This is why we need so many bookmaker accounts. We want to be in the position to take advantage of any prices that seem out of line to us.

Prices can be found in a range of places. *Pricewise* in the Racing Post is a good starting point. It highlights the prices from the main bookmakers for each horse for the main betting races of the day.

By the time we've done our studying though, these are likely to have changed, as the public start laying their bets. In particular, hyped horses – the ones tipsters have plugged will have shortened.

The next option I used for years was good old teletext and a pen and paper. You need to go to lots of pages but most major bookmakers have pages dedicated to their early odds.

These days I use the internet. There are a few sites that list up-to-date (relatively) prices for a range of bookies, notably www.oddschecker.co.uk and www.easyodds.com. In the heat of a Saturday they can get outdated quite quickly but they are a good starting-point.

Let's look at those World Cup bets again, but let's add the range of prices from all the bookmakers I have accounts with..

Team	My odds	general bookie odds	Range
Argentina	4/1	4/1	7/2 – 9/2
France	4/1	4/1	7/2 – 5/1
Italy	8/1	6/1	5/1 – 15/2
Portugal	10/1	11/1	10/1 – 14/1
Brazil	12/1	13/2	6/1 – 8/1
England	12/1	12/1	9/1 – 14/1
Spain	12/1	10/1	15/2 – 10/1
Germany	14/1	14/1	10/1 – 20/1

The following are all possible value (if I could get on in time), based on my odds and the best prices available.

Argentina	9/2
France	5/1
Portugal	14/1
England	14/1
Germany	20/1

Remarkably we have identified 5 possible value bets.

Ask yourself which of the following represents the best value, based on my 'true' odds and uncluttered by your own views of each team's chances:

Maybe that big looking 20/1 about Germany – a full 6 points more than my own odds? Or possibly the 5/1 about France? Difficult isn't it? Not according to an actuary I know "Simple really. You just relate your bet to the difference between true odds and offered odds, modified by the probable odds of winning." Hmm...

Luckily there is a fantastic mathematical formula for working out just how much value there is in the above 5 best prices. I did find it very confusing at first, but it is very easy once you get the hang of it, and I am again indebted to Nick Mordin for making it clear to me.

The Kelly Criterion

Basically, this clever chap called Kelly came up with an equation that shows that the amount you should bet should be determined by the certainty you feel about the result, and the relationship of that to the odds on offer. In other words, he has devised an equation that will tell us how much to bet depending on how our 'true odds' are shorter than the odds actually on offer.

The starting-point is that if you are 100% sure of the outcome you should bet 100% of your money regardless of the odds. If there's no value, you shouldn't bet at all. So, if you are only 50% sure of the outcome, and the odds on offer are odds-on, you shouldn't risk any of your money.

Overleaf is a table that does all the hard work for you, although it does not cover all the prices. Never mind. The best thing is to know how to calculate the edge yourself.

We will use the Portugal example above, where our 'true odds' are 10/1, but 14/1 is available

Step 1
Work out the chance that you think the team has in percentage terms. We have Portugal at 10/1, which equates to 9%

Step 2
Multiply this by the actual odds on offer.
Best odds on offer = 14/1. 9 x 14 = 126

Step 3
Subtract the probability that you think the horse has of losing. Portugal has a 9% chance of winning. Therefore, it has 91% chance of losing.
126 – 91 = 35

Step 4
Divide the resulting number by the offered odds.
The offered odds are 14/1. 35 divided by 14 = 2.5

The Kelly Criterion tells us that we should be putting 2.5% of our bank on   Portugal at odds of 14/1. We'll discuss using a bank in a later chapter and, rightly or wrongly, will modify Kelly's advice slightly.

For the moment let's practise on the other four teams.

Argentina
1.   My odds of 4/1 equate to 20%
2.   Best odds are 9/2. 20 x 4.5 = 90
3.   Odds for losing = 80%. 90-80 = 10
4.   Divided by available odds. 10 divided by 4.5 = 2.2
At 9/2 I should be risking 2.2% of my bank on Argentina

France
1.   My odds of 4/1 equate to 20%
2.   Best odds are 5/1. 20 x 5 = 100
3.   Odds for losing = 80%. 100-80 = 20
4.   Divided by available odds. 20 divided by 5 = 4
At 5/1 I should be risking 4% of my bank on France

England
1.   My odds of 12/1 equate to 7.7% (rounded down)
2.   Best odds are 14/1. 7.7 x 14 = 107.8
3.   Odds for losing = 92.3%. 107.8 - 92.3 = 15.5
4.   Divided by available odds. 15.5 divided by 14 = 1.1
At 14/1 I should be risking 1.1% of my bank on England

Germany
1.   My odds of 14/1 equate to 6.7%
2.   Best odds are 20/1. 6.7 x 20 = 134
3.   Odds for losing = 93.3%. 134 – 93.3 = 40.7
4.   Divided by available odds.   40.7 divided by 20 = 2
At 20/1 I should be risking 2% of my bank on Germany

So, our potential value looks as follows
France   4.0
Portugal   2.5
Argentina   2.2
Germany   2.0
England   1.1

Was this what you expected? This is what my actuarial friend
meant when he said 'modified by the actual chance of winning'.
The maths follows the rule of thumb that the bigger the value the
bigger the bet, but shows you how big that value is. Getting 5/1
about a 4/1 chance is bigger value than 20/1 about a 14/1 chance
because the formula takes into account the overall likelihood of the
bet winning. Whereas with the Germany bet you are getting a
much longer price, but a much longer price about something that
isn't very likely to happen at all.

This doesn't mean we've found a bet yet. But we have determined
what value exists. For what it's worth there isn't much there that
excites me. When the criteria tell me I should be putting on 10% of
my bank or more, then I start to get excited.

Let's go back to our racing example and put in the best odds available.

Horse	General odds	My odds	Best odds
Batswing	11/4	4/1	3/1
Victory Roll	5/1	6/1	11/2
Haditovski	11/2	9/2	7/1
~~Reggie Buck~~	6/1		
~~Carandrew~~	13/2		
~~Iris Collonges~~	7/1		
Marble Arch	12/1	9/1	14/1
Maximus	14/1	14/1	16/1

We now know that 14/1 to 16/1 (Maximus) is hardly worth noting (1.1% of bank). Haditovskii and Marble Arch are interesting though.

Haditovski
1. My percentage = 18.2%
2. Multiplied by best odds. 18.2 x 7 = 127.4
3. Minus odds of losing. 127.4 – 81.8 = 45.6
4. Divided by best odds. 45.6 divided by 7 = 6.5
We should put 6.5% of our bank on Haditovski at 7/1.

Marble Arch
1. My percentage = 10%
2. Multiplied by best odds. 10 x 14 = 140
3. Minus odds of losing. 140 – 90 = 50
4. Divided by best odds. 50 divided by 14 = 3.57
We should put 3.57% of our bank on Marble Arch at 14/1

The reason I made you go through a few examples is that, even with the table overleaf, this is a mathematical calculation that should come easily to you. It's one thing to be able to do it with the best morning odds, but we also want to be able to do it with real prices. Some horses can drift amazingly, either unwanted by the public, or forced out by a mass of money for one or two other runners, as the bookies try to balance their books.

What you should have in your book is a note against each potential value runner as to what that value is – ie Haditovski has 6.5 written along-side it.

Chapter 6 – Finding the right bets

("Miniver thought, and thought, and thought,
And thought about it." E A Robinson)

It may be as late as 11:00 and the best prices have gone (more on that later), and we haven't even decided on our bets yet. Good. Finding horses with a chance of winning is relatively easy. Recognising if there is any value in backing any of them is a huge step. But both are pointless if you fail to strike the right bets to make the most of the value you have identified.

There are a number of elements to this part of the process. We need to pick the right type of bets, we need to stake the optimum amount of money, and we need to manage our funds properly. Later chapters will consider staking and overall money management. For now, let's consider all the types of bets we could or should be making.

Single win bets

These are going to be our staple bet. Roughly half my bets are single win bets. Where we have identified one horse as being stand-out value we should back it to win. It's very easy to track your effectiveness at this sort of bet.

The only problem we are going to have is that we will have to face the probability of some very long losing streaks. I have often gone 30 single win bets in a row without picking a winner. The major reason for this is the value conundrum. As we have established the horses we are betting are the ones we believe to be at longer odds than their 'true' odds should be. As we have also established the favourite is usually over-bet by the public, and the bookie usually prices up the horse much shorter than it should be.

Which means it is relatively uncommon to be backing favourites. Our approach on the whole is to oppose them. This leads to backing horses at longer odds, for me averaging around the 8/1 – 10/1 mark. This will obviously lead to a reduced strike-rate than if we were backing evens money favourites all the time. My strike-rate on single win bets has stayed relatively constant over the years, varying between 15-20%. At that sort of strike-rate long losing runs are inevitable.

Here's an example of an obvious bet (of a losing one as it turned out).

Haydock Saturday 15 December 2001. Handicap Hurdle B class. 2m 4f 4 run – 3 circled - 90-95%

		A	B	C	
TRC/TS	Telemoss	9/4	5/4	10/11	1st
TF/RP3	Kates Charm	9/4	9/4	5/2	4th
TF/TRC/P	Aspirant Dancer	9/4	10/3	5/1	3rd

A = My prices
B = Early prices
C = Starting-price

I quite like races like this. Races with small fields can be tactical affairs, with little pace, and a sprint at the end. These three horses seem closely rated. Telemoss and Kates Charm do look like they could be too good for Aspirant Dancer, but he has plenty going for him as well. I balance his probable slight shortfall in ability with the fact he'll almost certainly be the pace setter. I don't have too much difficulty coming up with the solution that all of them can be given even chances, so I settle on 31% of the book for each – 9/4.

When I compare that with the Racing Post odds I see that they have taken a view, and installed Telemoss as a likely strong favourite. This isn't surprising. A quick glance at the Haydock Tipster Selection Box shows that Telemoss had 10 tips for it, Kate's Charm 3 and Aspirant dancer 2. (I didn't actually look at this box until after the race – I maybe should have done). If those odds are borne out in the actual market the only horse I would back would be Aspirant Dancer.

When I look at the early prices, things are even better. Telemoss is stronger and Aspirant Dancer weaker. 100/30 is available. Let's do the Kelly Criterion and follow the maths.

9/4 = a 31% chance. 31 x 3.33 = 103.23
Subtract chance of losing. 103.23 – 69 = 34.23
Divided by bookie's odds. 34.23 divided by 3.33 = 10.27
I should be putting 10% of my bank on Aspirant dancer.

As I've said we will look at bank management later. For now, let's say I should be putting 10 *'Kelly points'* on Aspirant Dancer to win.

That's an obvious single win bet, and is exactly what I did.

However, prior to the race Telemoss was even more in favour with the punters, and eventually went odds-on. As a result, Aspirant Dancer drifted to 5/1 as bookies looked for punters like me to help them balance their books. At 5/1 I should have been putting about 17 points onto Aspirant Dancer. I certainly should have topped up my bet at the bigger price, but I wasn't paying attention and missed my chance.

In the race itself Aspirant Dancer went off in front as expected. If anything, the jockey didn't do one thing or the other, he set off a good pace, but then allowed the rest of the field to close up as they liked coming towards two out. Telemoss took over, and was actually challenged by the horse I hadn't even considered, before holding on for a loudly-cheered half-length win by all those punters who had got odds-on about a horse I believed was only a 9/4 shot.

So, I lost 10 points of my bank. What did I learn? Maybe on reflection my pricing wasn't quite right. For a start, I'd under-estimated the horse I'd not even circled. And maybe I should have gone shorter on the favourite.

However, even if I priced it up again, with the twenty-twenty vision of hindsight, I'd still be betting something like:

Telemoss	7/4
Kates Charm	5/2
Aspirant Dancer	3/1

If I am cross about anything it's that I didn't take the time to consider that Aspirant Dancer was a probable drifter. Overall I'm happy with the bet I struck.

Let's have a quick look at another example. I've said above that it's unusual to back the favourite but here's an example where the favourite seemed the obvious choice to me.

Royal Ascot – Group 1   3 year old fillies. 13 run. 5 circled – top 5 in market. 70%

		My odds	Best odds
NM/CW/Trends/J	Banks Hill	7/2	5/1
	Ameerat	6/1	5/1
TS/J	Crystal Music	6/1	4/1
TF/J	Rose Gypsy	8/1	7/1
TF	Monnavanna	12/1	10/1

This race is a no-brainer. Banks Hill looks to have a cracking chance on form, and has Nick Mordin and Clive Weight and 10 year trends all tipping it up. The only issue would be whether there is any value. I didn't look at any prices when I priced it up, and was amazed to find that Banks Hill was on offer at a remarkable 5/1, with all the other horses a point or two shorter than my estimates. Ok, there's not great value there. Something like 6 points. But it is a completely obvious single win bet, and an example of finding a good priced favourite. I got this one right. Banks Hill put up probably the best performance of the meeting. She then went on to win at the Breeders Cup at ridiculously long odds.

The only thing to decide is what your minimum value should be before you do a win single. I'll modify this in later chapters, but for now a good rule of thumb is to only strike a bet of the value recommended by the Kelly Criterion where it equals a bet of 4 Kelly points or more. Going back to the World Cup bets that would mean although five teams represent value, only one really justifies a bet, and that's France.

Split win bets

Things will not always be so clear–cut. As I've said about half my bets are single win bets. About a quarter of my bets are what I call split win bets. Basically, this means backing more than one horse in a race, usually two.

Again, the value quotient will be your guide.

There are usually two types of race where you can end up with split win bets. The first is where you have taken a stand against one or two of the favourites, to the extent that you haven't even circled them. In doing so, you're almost bound to find some nice-priced horses.

Here's an example:

Cheltenham Friday 14 December 2001   3m 2f B Class
Handicap Chase. 11 run - 6 circled 75%

		RP price	My odds
	~~Beau~~	4/1	
TF/PW	Frenchman's Creek	6/1	5/1(7/2F)
	~~Royal Predica~~	6/1	
	Smarty	6/1	7/1
TS	Eau De Cologne	7/1	7/1(11/1)
~~TRC~~	Earthmover	8/1	10/1
TF/GD/TRC/Lad	Royale de Vassey	8/1	5/1(11/1)
~~TF~~	Samuel Wilderspin	9/1	10/1

This looked a great race to me. I couldn't have Beau at any price.
You get to know the chasers over the years, and I like to think I
have a good feel for Beau. For me he needs to dominate, and needs
a real distance. I crossed his name out without a second's thought.
I didn't even need to know that the stable was hopelessly out of
form, or add that it's is virtually impossible for horses to win these
longer-distance big handicaps off top-weight. I was astonished
when I found out he was favourite.

Royal Predica (with the benefit of hindsight) was a somewhat
dodgier decision. Looking back at the form I imagine I crossed him
out on grounds of distance, but he was hardly proven not to stay.
Whatever, I had two of the first three in the market crossed-out.
Given that my book on circled runners is based on 75%, and on
bookies' prices Beau and Royal Predica are worth around 35% it
would be surprising if I couldn't find some value.

The most obvious horse is Royal de Vassey who is a stand-out bet
at 8/1. That represents around 6 points on the Kelly Criterion.
Imagine my surprise then when I see that he's 11/1 with Corals –

more like a hefty 9 point bet. Such was the stand-out I actually stopped what I was doing ran upstairs and tried to get on at 11/1. It had all gone of course, but I did get 9/1, against a starting-price of 7/1.

When I came back downstairs and resumed my study it was clear there was another horse at value – Frenchman's Creek. It's usual for one of the circled favourites to be value in this circumstance, and I have to say I really fancied Frenchman's Creek as the likely winner. However, the Kelly Criterion value of 6/1 about a 5/1 chance is only 2.8. Worse still, the Pricewise column has tipped him up, and the 6/1 disappeared round about the time I was tucking into my second chocolate croissant. The horse eventually went off unbacked 7/2 favourite.

Eau de Cologne (who I can't say I fancied much, even though he had won nicely for me the season before)., didn't appear to be value until I looked at the best prices on oddschecker and saw that he was a remarkable 11/1 with Ladbrokes. That's 4.5 points on the Kelly Criterion. So, there's two horses at more than 4 points value, and so I backed them both. For the record Eau De Cologne ran as badly as I might have anticipated. Royale de Vassey won nicely, but only after a fierce struggle with the uncircled Royal Predica. Beau ran a stinker. Frenchman's Creek was a creditable third.

I could have had my fingers burnt, but instead enjoyed a nice profit. I'll leave you to decide whether I was astute, or a lucky muppet, or somewhere in between. Crossing out favourites is a dangerous business, but potentially a very rewarding one.

The second type of race is probably more common. This is where there is a competitive field, with no value in the favourites, but a couple of eye-catching prices about a couple of middle-ranged or long-priced horses. Often these prices are stand-out prices with one or two bookmakers.

Here's another winning example
Royal Ascot Group 2   1m 4f   8 run – 6 circled at 95%

		Early prices	My odds
J/TF/85/TS/GD	Mutafaweq	5/2	3/1
J/TF/84/RP3	Wellbeing	7/4	3/1
TF/J	Zindabad	16/1	9/1
	Adilabad	8/1	9/1
CW/J/ TRC	Lucido	6/1	5/1
TF/P	Sandmason	14/1	9/1

The pace seemed the key to me when considering this race. Mutafaweq and Wellbeing have loads going for them, and are clearly the best contenders. They both boast good speed figures, and look like they'd appreciate a decent pace enabling them to use their class. And it looked like that may be a problem. There was no guaranteed pace. The two who had bits and pieces in their favour were Zindabad and Sandmason. The latter in particular is not only a horse I like a lot as being tough and genuine, but looked like he could steal this race from the front. He was also the stable's second string behind Wellbeing. I often find that once a jockey has made his choice about which of the two horses he will be riding, the bookies push the second string to a far longer price than they should be.

When I looked at the best prices both horses had a couple of firms going very long on them. Zindabad at 16/1 equals 4.3 Kelly points, and Sandmason equals 3.57 Kelly points. Given my rule of thumb earlier of a minimum of 4 Kelly points my bet should have been to just back Zindabad. But I hope you can see that backing them both seems obvious.

With single wins making up about 50% of my bets and split wins about 25%, the rest represent at most only a quarter of the bets I make. Single win bets and split bets are your staple – you want to be grinding out your 10% profit from these bets. The remaining bets are either variations on the above, or they are designed to be the icing on the cake, the occasional big wins, get rich quick bets.

Each way singles

The list of hand-me-down wisdom regarding betting goes something like this.

- It's a mug's game
- All gamblers are losers
- You'll never meet a broke bookie
- All racing is fixed
- If you must have a bet, go each way.

For decades, I've been watching the once a year punters do their quid each way on the Grand National, jump up and down like demented puppies when their well-backed favourite comes third, and then shake their head in disbelief as they go to collect their £3 in winnings, including their stake.

At the dogs, I've often seen people put a couple of quid each way on a very short-priced dog, which has then come second. They've roared it on, received the slaps on the back from their mates and gone off to collect their winnings. When they return, they whisper that they think they may have been ripped off, as they've actually got back less than they put on.

I blame my mum for my on-going affair with each way betting, (she blames a trace of gypsy blood for my 'affliction'). When she took me to the Derby at a tender age she let me back a horse called

Relkino at what I believe to be enormous odds of 33/1 (probably more like 16/1). When she went to put the bet on, I remember she was embarrassed and she and the bookie laughed dismissively at my choice. All the money was for Wollow – an odds-on certainty. Well, I can't tell you who won, but I can tell you it wasn't Wollow, and that Relkino came second. Thus was born my passion for outsiders and my aversion to short-priced horses, and a general affection for each way bets.

For a few years, each way betting on long-priced horses was my most successful strategy. Indeed, my only strategy. Especially at the big meetings where I enjoyed a number of superb results.

And yet this latest flat season my records show that I made just one each way bet. It lost. I like to think I bet much more professionally now. But, I don't really consider myself someone who should be giving advice on this subject. You'll have to work out what's most profitable for you.

The main reason I have virtually stopped doing each way bets is the increase in the number of split wins I make. Essentially instead of one nice priced horse to win or place, I found I was better off picking two nice priced horses to win.

The other reason is I don't really know when each way represents value nor how much to stake. When the Kelly method tells me I should be putting 4 points to win on a selection, and I have it in my head that at 33/1 I really should be backing each way, I don't know whether to go 2 points each way, or 4 points each way, or some funny combination – 3 points win, 1 point place and so on.

Each way rules offer one fifth the odds for most races, but one quarter odds in races of 5 –7 runners, and in handicaps of 16 runners and over.

The rule of thumb I seem to have abandoned but which held me in good stead was that at one quarter odds a place you shouldn't bet each way at under 16/1, and at a fifth odds a place you shouldn't bet each way at 20/1. I've no real idea why I came up with those cut-off points but they served me well over the years. I think it had something to do with returns of 4 times stake.

And that's another thing. Something to do when you strike an each way bet. The great gambling books say that you must consider the each way bet as two separate bets, the win single which you treat as normal, and a separate place bet where you have worked out the value price In a horse being placed. Completely true. But not something I've ever been able to do. The best I can do is remember that when the horse is placed you need to take into account the losing win single when determining your profit. This provides me with a rule of thumb for determining value that helps ensure I don't bet each way lightly.

Say a hose is 20/1 at quarter odds the place. If I place a tenner each way on the horse and it runs second I get £60 back. That looks a nice return for a tenner place bet – 5/1. However, rightly or wrongly I always treat it as a twenty pound bet. Suddenly it's only a 2/1 bet. Looking at it in those terms, with the win bet being some sort of unlikely bonus, helps ensure you only go each way when you are sure there is value.

Times when each way betting could well be value would include

a) Rogues and gentlemen
When the horse is difficult to win with, but often runs into a place. This would include genuine horses just not quite good enough for their class – you see this a lot in Group and Listed races. It also includes highly talented animals who for some reason won't go through with their final challenge, and come second. Horses are priced to win, and so can be easily given a dismissive 25/1 about

winning (5/1 the place), but actually have a really strong likelihood of coming second or third.

In the big races, you can often cross out a horse without a second's thought for certain races when considering whether it is good enough to win – Go Ballistic in the Gold Cup for example. But when you ask yourself whether it could sit off the furious place, hunt around for a couple of circuits, and pick off the horses that have gone off too fast, or who don't truly get 3 miles and 2 furlongs at Cheltenham, you begin to think that a place is well within reach. 66/1 seems hardly long enough for him to win, 16/1 a place looks huge. Even working out the value by accounting for the win bet (which is roughly 7/1) it still looks huge.

b) the number of runners
Certain races offer much better value than others.
Here's a table comparing true mathematical odds for a horse to be placed compared to bookie's odds based on fifth or quarter odds. Note where there could be in-built value.

Bookmaker's Odds				
Number of Runners	Places Covered	True Odds	Quarter Odds	Fifth Odds
5	1-2	1.5/1	1.0/1	0.8/1
6	1-2	2.0/1	1.3/1	1.0/1
7	1-2	2.5/1	1.5/1	1.2/1
8	1-2-3	1.7/1	1.8/1	1.4/1
9	1-2-3	2.0/1	2.0/1	1.6/1
10	1-2-3	2.3/1	2.3/1	1.8/1
11	1-2-3	2.7/1	2.5/1	2.0/1
12	1-2-3	3.0/1	2.8/1	2.2/1
13	1-2-3	3.3/1	3.0/1	2.4/1
14	1-2-3	3.7/1	3.3/1	2.6/1
15	1-2-3	4.0/1	3.5/1	2.8/1
16	1-2-3-4	3.0/1	3.8/1	3.0/1
17	1-2-3-4	3.3/1	4.0/1	3.2/1
18	1-2-3-4	3.5/1	4.3/1	3.4/1
19	1-2-3-4	3.8/1	4.5/1	3.6/1
20	1-2-3-4	4.0/1	4.8/1	3.8/1
21	1-2-3-4	4.3/1	5.0/1	4.0/1

Obviously, a 5 runner race offering quarter odds on the first two gives you a better mathematical chance of success than a 7 runner race offering the same. An 8 runner race offering a fifth odds the first three gives you a much better chance of getting placed than a fifth the first three in a 15 runner race.

16 runners and above though will have the problem of huge over-rounds getting in the way of there being any value.

One thing to look out for, usually at Festivals, is where bookies make a concession and go quarter odds all races, regardless of numbers of runners.

c) Opposing short-priced favourites
I like long-priced horses in uncompetitive fields, where there are one, maybe two really short-priced horses. My own speciality is novice chases, where I like to take on odds-on horses who haven't proven themselves, opposing them with horses who are either unexposed from decent trainer's stables, or with horses that have proven themselves sound jumpers, who preferably like to front-run.

d) Topweights
Over the jumps, topweights in top-class handicaps really struggle to win. In the final stages the weight gets to them, and they get out-paced. However, their class and proven jumping ability at speed, often allows them to run into a place at a nice price.

On the flat there are a number of horses that get caught in a twilight zone – where they are not good enough to win top listed races, but too high in the weights to win handicaps. As above, in top-class handicaps with guaranteed pace, they can often plug on into a nice-priced third or fourth.

e) Speed figures
My own speed ratings are very good at identifying horses that can run well at the major festivals. Getting a speed rating from me means they've run really well in a really fast race. Races at the Festivals are always run at a furious pace, and my figures tell me which horses like that style of race.

A similar profile is the horses that love the end to end gallop of strongly-run competitive races. On both the flat and in 2m hurdles you see the same horses run really well in cavalry charges that make up the big handicaps, often at great prices.

If you don't intend to do your own speed ratings, you could always collate and collect Dave Edwards ratings from the Weekender each week. A rating of 50 and above should equate to my speed figures. It's worth keeping a list because the form pages only ever give the highest rating and the latest rating.   I like to know how many high ratings a horse has – a few ratings is about the best indicator of a genuine class horse that I can think of.

You could easily add an 'alternative handicapping' mark alongside any horse that was advantaged by any of the above factors, and build it into your analysis. The only caveat I would apply is remember that you may have crossed a horse out as being incapable of winning, but it may well be capable of placing, so you shouldn't just consider your circled horses when considering value for a place.

Forecasts (Exactas)

Forecasts are bets on two or more horses to come first and second, either in a specified order, or in any order. There are two types, those offered by bookmakers – called forecasts, and those offered by the Tote called exactas.

My rule of thumb is, if the forecast includes the favourite or short-priced second favourite bet with the bookmakers, otherwise always bet via the Tote. Given the sort of odds I like it won't surprise you to know that all the exactas I placed last season were on the Tote.

There are four main times when I use forecasts.

a) Split single wins.

When I've backed two horses in a race, normally at nice odds, I almost always do a small (1 or 2 points) combination exacta on the two horses. It's an icing on the cake bet, but one with a chance of great returns, and a thrill. You only need a couple of these to come in during a season (and believe me, that's all you'll get), to transform your fund price.

You can decide how much to stake on a bastardisation of the Kelly method. Very roughly forecasts pay out on a multiplication of the two horses' starting-prices. Two 10/1 horses should pay out around 100/1. You can use that to assess overall value. So, taking Zindabad and Sandmason in the race we looked at earlier when discussing split win singles:

Their combined odds at likely starting price = 12/1 x 14/1 = roughly 165/1
Their combined odds at my 'real' prices = 9/1 x 9/1 = 80/1
You can apply the Kelly method to that and it will say you should put roughly 0.65 points on the forecast.

I didn't bother this time (for a reason we'll look at below), but I wish I had have done, and decided in the future to do at least a one point combination exacta regardless, and more if the Kelly criterion told me to.

b) Same trainer

Where I have decided to back a trainer's second string horse in a race, I now have a rule whereby I have to do a combination forecast with it and the stable's first string, as long as the first string's price isn't ridiculously short – (say less than 2/1). This bet's

114

been very kind to me – especially with the larger stables of Pipe, Johnston, Cecil and Henderson. There's no science behind it, but I pass it on anyway.

It cost me in the Sandmason/Zindabad race though. Sandmason and Wellbeing were both from the Cecil stable, and so I had to do the forecast on the two. That's what prevented me from doing the second forecast on Sandmason and Zindabad. When we look at psychology and bank management we'll see how that was a mistake. I should have covered my bases more thoroughly.

c) Three 'small value' horses.
Often when you've priced a race up, you'll find no clear single win bet, and not even a split single bet. You may find bits and pieces of value – in the under 4 Kelly points range. If you have three such horses, then I suggest your bet on that race is a combination forecast on the three horses. This represents 6 bets, so you need to make sure that the minimum pay-out makes that worthwhile. I set a minimum pay-out on any combination of 50/1.

I'd reduce this if it was a race where I had uncircled favourites and short-priced horses, and really wanted to get at the race, but for some reason couldn't find sufficient value. This can happen occasionally in large handicaps where the bookies overround is 145% or higher and any sort of value is thin on the ground.

d) A strong value horse and a small-value outsider
Often there's a clear single win horse where I want to oppose a favourite, or a few short-priced horses. Usually it's fairly short-priced itself, but a big value bet of 15 Kelly points or more. There's also an outsider at small value – below 4 points – say 14/1 instead

of 16/1. That horse isn't worth becoming part of a split single bet, but it is worth doing a forecast on it to come second. My head tells me to just do the one forecast with the strong horse to win and the other to come second. My heart tells me that if the outsider actually came to win I'd be a gibbering mass of red wine stains for months to come. So, do a combination forecast, possibly with higher stakes on the more likely result.

Win doubles

'Punters' are addicted to multiple bets – Patents, Yankees, Lucky 15s, Super Yankees, Canadians, Heinz 57. Betting shops love to advertise their latest "Super-Duper-Bet-A-Minute-Roll-up-Roll-over-Across The Card-All-Action-Accumulator (with 10% consolation for 1 winner). Super Bets. For *them*.

Take a Yankee. Four horses in six doubles, four trebles and an accumulator. The first horse loses. That's seven bets lost on the first race. Bollocks to that.

One horse wins, at a nice price, say 6/1. Your returns. Zilch. Whereas if you'd backed them all in win singles you'd have a return of 175%. With that sort of return you can forget Saturday gambling and start thinking about that yacht in St Tropez.

It's the number of multiples that kills you in the end. You haven't just got the doubles, but the trebles and four-folds and so on. For people who love multiples I always say just do doubles and an accumulator. So, for 5 horses, instead of the 26 bets of the Canadian, do 10 doubles at two and half times the Canadian stake. And a 1 point accumulator (each way if you must). Two winners is a good strike-rate for a Canadian. The returns from two winners will be vastly higher this way. Three winners in a Canadian and they'll probably declare a national holiday. But actually the returns from the doubles method probably won't be much different, and you'll still have the accumulator.

Let's take three winners 2/1, 4/1 and 6/1.

Your £1 Canadian will pay three doubles and a treble as follows:
£15 + £21 + £35 + £105 = 176

Your £2.50 win doubles will pay three doubles as follows:
£37.50 + £52.50 + £87.50 = £177.50

Don't worry about the four folds because that's never going to happen in your life-time, unless you're backing favourites. Obviously, neither's the accumulator, but we're all allowed one point 'dream' bets. The problem with the Canadian (with its 5 four folds and a five-fold) is you're wasting 6 points on 'dream' bets.

So, stick to win doubles. You can do a load of them if you must. If you do and you want to know how many bets it is, there's a n easy way to know. Simply multiply the number of horses you want to double up, by one less than the number of horses and divide by two.

4 horses = 4 x 3 divided by 2 = 6 doubles
6 horses = 6 x 5 divided by 2 = 15 doubles
8 horses = 8 x 7 divided by 2 = 28 doubles
and so on

Personally, I've stopped doing lots of doubles. Past records have shown me the error of my ways. These day I concentrate on just the win double – ie two horses only, to a bigger stake. These I treat as my 'story' bets. They are a view of the day's racing as a whole as opposed to the race by race analysis we have been undertaking so far. Usually these jump out at me. And usually they are trainer doubles. There are a few others as well and I've outlined the common ones below.

a) Trainer win doubles

A trainer sends two horses to a meeting. They look to have cracking chances, both circled and with lots going for them, probably including the trainer being bang in form, or having a great record at the track. They are value or border-line value bets. You may be backing one, or both in win singles, or they may be just not quite value enough to warrant a bet in their own right. But you feel you can almost read tomorrow's headlines – "Johnston lands both the big prizes." If you want, you can work out the Kelly value points for doubles, but you'll be dealing in some fairly unwieldy figures. I'd probably save yourself the trouble and do the double to a set amount – 5 Kelly points for me currently.

I limit myself to making sure the trainer has only two horses at the meeting. I used to get enticed into throwing in the third horse, or fourth horse and ending up in multiple-land as discussed above.

The trainer may also have two horses across cards that jump out at you – maybe good horses in the two big races of the day. The situation that would interest me is where I find I'm backing the least fancied of these two horses in a win single. There's me backing the 10/1 shot in the big race at Doncaster and feeling good about it as a bet, when the stable jockey has gone to Sandown to ride a 3/1 favourite. I'd have to give the jockey some credit and do a win double on those two horses.

b) Jockey doubles

Exactly the same as the above but focusing on jockeys. I may not limit myself to them only having two rides that day. What I'm looking at is eye-catching rides on two circled horses. Maybe they're a top jockey riding away from their yard. Or they maybe they have come over from Ireland or France and picked up a couple of notable rides for unexpected stables.

c) 'Saver doubles'

Quite often when you have listed all your alternative handicapping factors you will have a couple of horses in races who look to have great chances- ie they are easily the most obvious winners. Unfortunately, you can't get value on either of them, no matter how you try. You're probably actually opposing them with better value horses that have much less chance of winning. I suggest you account for the obvious and do the double to cover yourself. This goes right against the mantra of value, but is an important part of dealing with the psychological side of gambling.

My longest-serving syndicate member often accuses me of looking 'too hard' for value, and he's right. These are a way of re-dressing the balance.

There's no limit to the ideas behind these sorts of bets. They should represent a small part of your betting armoury. They're for after you've looked at each race in turn and isolated your core bets for the day. They are about you looking at the day's racing as a whole, and saying – 'what's the story here?' Or 'what stands out overall?'

Any of your alternative handicapping methods may scream out win double at you. For example, you notice how short Ladbrokes are on two circled runners in the day's two big races. They're nearly twice as long with Hills. Grab your chance and do a win double at the Hills prices.

Each way doubles

Everything I said about each way bets above stands here. I can't help feeling there's a great bet here I'm not exploiting and I intend to investigate ways of making the most from it over the coming years. I haven't found the key to it yet though.

Placepot

The placepot (a Tote multiple bet where you get paid a dividend for picking horse(s) to be placed in the first 6 races on the card) can be a recommended bet in the right circumstances.

It's especially useful as a psychological tool. Some Saturday's you may find you've done your two to three hours of studying only to come up with one or two bets. You're going to feel cheated, and the temptation will be to have a few more bets anyway – for the action. One good way to let all your work count for something would be to do a placepot to small stakes selecting quite a few horses overall. This should give you an interest in the day's racing and satisfy your craving, as long as you don't lose out in the first race.

The problem is you will almost certainly not have studied all the races, as you will have crossed some of them out before you started. My rule of thumb is to do the placepot only where I have studied at least four of the races. I would be very conservative in my selections in the races I hadn't studied - for example picking the first two favourites.

I'm attracted to the placepot where I have three or more races where I have few circled runners. Normally you'll have quite a few races where you have circled more than 6 runners. Deciding which ones to include in your placepot is problematical. One decent deciding factor is to look at their ratio of places to runs and insisting on at least 50% placed.

But where I have looked at races where there doesn't seem to be too many circled horses, and especially where I am opposing a few short-priced horses, the placepot suddenly looks very inviting. I normally end up with 48 to 100 lines and will spend between 5 – 10 points in total on such a bet.

To calculate the number of lines simply multiply the number of horses chosen in each race. Normal examples:

2 x 2 x 1 x 3 x 2 x 2 = 48 LINES
2 x 2 x 2 x 2 x 2 x 2 = 64 LINES
2 x 4 x 2 x 1 x 1 x 3 = 48 LINES
2 x 3 x 1 x 3 x 2 x 2 = 72 LINES
2 x 2 x 3 x 2 x 2 x 2 = 96 LINES
2 x 3 x 4 x 1 x 2 x 2 = 96 LINES
and so on.

Finding one horse (and not the favourite) in a race helps enormously in limiting the number of lines, at least until it finishes fourth in a three-way photo.

The down-side of the placepot is that the pay-out depends on what other horses fill the places. It's only any good when the favourites get beaten. I remember going to Kempton with some non-gambling friends and one of them had done a one line £1 placepot (a frankly ridiculous bet, as I told him). So, naturally he won. His problem was, although he was peeing his pants with excitement, his carefully chosen placepot was actually the six favourites. We were forced to wait for twenty minutes after the last race whilst he queued up with knee-trembling anticipation for his winning dividend which eventually came to the princely sum of £7 and tuppence. Which he promptly spent in petrol in the queue to leave the car park.

The very worst thing with the placepot is when you win it the hard way – getting three or four 20/1 shots into the frame, say, but your work is undone by all the short-priced horses finishing in the frame as well, for a pathetic pay-out.

The one time you must do the placepot is at the Cheltenham festival. You'll have studied every race, the pools are enormous, and on the Tuesday and Thursday completely impossible. You won't win anything, but it's tradition. For the last 5 years, I haven't even got past the Triumph Hurdle, which is the first race on the Thursday, even though one year I put 7 horses in that race.

There are also the Jackpot and the Scoop6 which are similar but much harder as you have to pick the winning, rather than just placed horses in 6 named races. I have a fantastic strike-rate on the Jackpot. I've only done it about 10 times, and won three times. If the Jackpot isn't won on any day it rolls over to another meeting. After a festival, or other difficult meetings, the roll-over can reach huge sums – even a million pounds. Then I have a go.

I remember roping in colleagues at work for one really tasty roll-over. We each put in a tenner, and got the results through the afternoon, managing to stay in. Our problem was odds-on favourites won three of the races, so everyone else was still in as well. We landed the Jackpot but because of the low dividend and the number of lines we'd done, I handed each of them back £5.70 in return for their tenner.

On Saturdays, the Jackpot has been replaced by the Scoop6 which is the same idea but based mainly on Channel 4's TV races and costing a minimum of £2 per line. I've never done it. At £2 a line you either do just a few lines, which is the equivalent of doing the lottery, or you put together a syndicate willing to spend a grand or so each week chasing it.

Chapter 8 – Money Management

("I'll have a tenner on the winner, each way.")

The longest year of my life was the 6 months I spent at Tesco as a management trainee. I was only a bits and pieces gambler then. For a start, I was too poor to be wasting money. Small wins meant a lot to me. I remember the excitement at landing a £2 win double on Slip Anchor in the Derby and Oh So Sharp in the Oaks at something like 7/4 and 6/4.

So, it was with amazement that I used to listen to a couple of the warehouse boys re-tell their adventures at Wimbledon dogs of a Saturday night. These lads were only 19 or 20 years old, and earned at best £100 a week, and yet were boasting of the 'ton' they'd dropped on some dozy 3 dog in the 9:15.

There may have been some bravado behind their stories, but frankly I was pretty impressed.

When I left Tesco for bar-work the South London pub had its share of small-time criminals who liked nothing better than having a healthy punt. The Bar Manager would send me over to the bookies on a Saturday afternoon, with bets based on the tip-offs he'd had from his gangster mates. I gave this extra credence after one night when the barrow boys came in with a trophy their dog had just won them at Catford dogs. Taking my time cleaning their ash-tray, I heard them explain to a mate how their dog had won – 'we'd done the other 5' they laughed. One of them won so much money on Hallo Dandy winning the National he took himself off on a cruise.

One Friday, the guvnor gave me one of their tips and £50 to run across the road and put it on as soon as the horse drifted to 7/4 (certain that it would). I'd just been paid, £78 for a 65 hour week. I put it all on the horse as well. It won. Christ, was that exciting. Pant-staining exciting. I shake now when I remember it.

If you want to bet like that – good luck to you. This book won't help. This book is the equivalent of a recovery programme compared to that sort of adrenaline-pumping white-knuckle ride gambling. It's methadone to a heroin addict. It's a sterilised, sanitised version of punting that puts nothing at risk but your pride.

And the reason is my desperate affair with the Cheltenham Festival. Even ten years ago I was able to grind out a profit most seasons. I've since improved dramatically. But every March Cheltenham would come along and ruin it all. Don't get me wrong. I love Cheltenham. I start thinking about in November, when I've already isolated all 6 winners of the Royal and Sun Alliance Chase. I start doing 'get rich' accumulators long before Christmas on 33/1 chances for the Champion Hurdle, Queen Mum and Gold Cup.

Come February and I've started putting some good money down on my season's winners. By the time of the Festival I've already several hundred pounds invested in wads of betting-slips, half-full of horses long since injured or dead, or waiting for Aintree, or running in a different race, or just plain useless.

By the time the Champion Hurdle's been run on the Tuesday each and every one of these slips is offered up in sacrifice to the God of Cleeve Hill. It's hard to describe how hopeless my record is at Cheltenham except to say I went three complete years in the mid-nineties betting on every single one of the races that make up the festival, and never once backed a winner. 60 races.

And my bets were decent bets on the whole, supplemented by sphincter-tightening bets of ridiculous proportions. On the Wednesday that Ask Tom came second in the Queen Mum I'd done my bollocks. Three enormous bets, and I'd lost the equivalent of my entire betting bank and more. The bank I'd been building up slowly year after year. The bank I was so proud of I felt could call myself a semi-professional gambler.

After racing I sat on a bench up on Cleeve Hill as the lights glowed down below me and for three hours I shook. In my jacket pocket I had an empty hip-flask and a notebook I'd started with such optimism after the Tote hurdle at Chepstow the previous October. I threw the notebook away and vowed never to bet on tilt again.

So, you can say I take money management pretty seriously.

This is the most important chapter in the book. Don't argue with anything in it. Just do it. Much of it is linked to the psychological aspects that follow on in the next chapter.

There are essentially three elements. Maintaining a bank, keeping records and staking.

The bank.

1. This must be separate from your other money.
2. This must be money you do not need for anything else.

The best way to think of your bank is as a unit trust. It's a savings vehicle that invests in betting, and you are the Fund manager. You can top-up, pay in monthly, withdraw, take dividends, but you have to be able to track how well or badly you are doing bet by bet.

The bank can be any amount. I'd suggest a minimum of £500. A good starting-place is to relate the size of your bank to the average bet you currently make.

If you bet in fivers your bank should be £1000
If you bet in tenners your bank should be £2000

And so on, with your average bet-size representing just 0.5% of your bank.

Half per cent bets seem small. Certainly, most gambling books talk of much larger bets – 50 bet banks are quite common (2%), and even 25 bet banks (4%). As far as I'm concerned their advice is plain wrong. Even if you back short-priced horses. Firstly, a basic losing streak would decimate a 25 bet bank. Secondly, they do not take enough consideration of having to cope with long losing (and winning) streaks.

On a Saturday, we might be having ten bets or more. If our average bet was say 3% of the fund, we could well be putting 30% of the bank on the line on a Saturday. Complete losing days are not uncommon. How will you feel if you've lost a third of your money in one day? You'd need balls of steel to not be on tilt.

Our average bet will be roughly 0.5% of the bank, but we may go to 1% or higher on occasion (depending on the Kelly Criterion as we'll see later). A complete losing day could easily cost us 5% of our bank. Two bad Saturdays and we could be 10% down. Believe me that affects how you think, and how you bet. But we'll be able to cope with a 10% loss without losing control. At least I can.

And the same is true of big wins. With higher proportionate bets, a couple of big wins will have your bank shooting up. You'll get above yourself, you'll believe you've got this game cracked, and embark on a disastrous losing-run of over-staked bets on bare-value selections. Even with this most conservative bank management strategy I still have losing runs following-on from nice wins as a matter of inevitability. But at least this way I minimise the risk.

When you have decided on your bank, you need to put that money into a separate bank account. This account should have a debit card, so that you can do phone bets or internet bets directly from the account. Or if you bet exclusively on the High Street, keep it in cash in your sock drawer. Whatever, keep it separate.

The chances are your fund will never dip below 70 (I've been to 73), so in theory you won't actually need 70% of the money. Trust me, you still want it there. If you don't want it sat in the bank earning nothing in interest, do something else with it. Half of my bank is in Premium Bonds. I can get at the money if I need to, I get some nice little £50 bonuses from time to time, which either give the fund a wee kick, or pay expenses, and I find Premium Bonds in the spirit of the fund. The rest is split between the bank account and credit in my internet betting accounts. I have about £1800 currently just sat in various bookies' accounts earning them interest. Not best advice, but I like being able to place bets without having to deposit money first.

After I'd been wiped out at Cheltenham I started again with a £500 bank, a humbling amount, way below what I'd just lost. This is a bit misleading though, because in the first month I had a big win on a lucky forecast, which took it closer to £2000. I immediately 're-based' the fund, so it would be more accurate to say I started again with a £2000 fund.

This currently stands at £12000 (£1500 of which is friend's money). If some of you are disappointed both at the size of my fund and the size of my profits I suggest this game isn't for you, and you take up something easier – safe-breaking perhaps. Going from £2000 to £12000 in four years (8 seasons) certainly beats any other savings and investment vehicles I've got. My fund's the best performing Unit Trust in my portfolio. By miles.

Of those eight seasons, two have been sensational, three have seen slow-grinding profits, one was a disaster turned into brilliance with one win double and two have made small losses. And I've had some great fun along the way. I haven't had the bowel-emptying terror and excitement of a huge Cheltenham bet, but I have had some great days when the fund has shot-up on the back of some fantastic racing. I've had bad months when everything has seemed a waste of time and I've doubted my own judgement, but I've never come close to needing a park-bench and a hip-flask. I'm as close to being in control as I have ever been, and it's great.

Let's say you start with £2000. You need to set up your fund. To do this you want to divide your initial fund into units. I suggest £1 per unit. You are now the proud owner of 2000 units, with a current price of £1 per unit. Why not make your spouse or loved one a unit-holder as well – give him or her a stake in your fund. Or do it with a mate. (Reasons why in the Psychology chapter).

You want to set rules for the running of the fund (particularly if anyone else is involved). I suggest you have an end date for that fund (you may well roll the fund over to the next season). My end dates are the Sandown Whitbread meeting for the end of the jumps, and the Breeders Cup for the end of the flat. This does mean you'll be mixing flat and jumps at the ends of each season, but that doesn't matter much.

I suggest a spreadsheet is going to help, but you can do it on paper with a calculator. Set up a sheet that enables you to write down each bet, and that will update your unit price after each bet.

Staking

You've decided on the size of you bank, and set-it up as a separate pool of money. You've decided on your bet types, the end date of your fund, and have set up your first spreadsheet.

All you need to do is decide on how much you are going to be staking on each type of bet.

This is where our old friend the Kelly Criterion comes in. We have so far talked about Kelly's method as advising how many Kelly points to put on. Kelly of course originally meant those points to actually represent that percentage of your bank. So with France to win the World Cup I should be betting 4% of my bank at 5/1, when I believe the 'true' odds to be 4/1. With a £12000 bank that would mean a £360 bet.

A 17 point bet on Aspirant dancer once it had drifted to 5/1 would have meant a £2040 bet. Hmm. I think rightly or wrongly we need to be more conservative.

I came to use Kelly only a couple of seasons ago, and I love it. Prior to that I was betting roughly around half per cent of bank, or units as we have seen. Kelly has enabled me to range my betting more efficiently. But for psychological reasons, I have bastardised Kelly so that it maintains an average around the half per cent mark. Currently my fund is valued at £12000 and has 10000 units. A half per cent bet = £60 if based on the fund price and £50 if based on units. All I had to do was find the sort of value bets under the Kelly Criterion that I would previously have called decent bets. Two stood out.

A bet at 5/1 about a horse I think should be 3/1 results in a bet of 10 Kelly points.

A bet of 8/1 about a horse I think should be 4/1 also results in a bet of 10 Kelly points.

That makes it very easy. For single win bets and split win bets all I do is find out what the Kelly points are for each bet and multiply by 6 or 5 depending on whether I'm playing loose or tight (see next chapter), and round up or down to the nearest £5.

4 Kelly points is usually my minimum bet, so for the France bet I would be staking either £20 or £25.

Aspirant Dancer at 17 Kelly points would be a bet of between £85 and £105. The most Kelly points I have come up with so far is 7/4 about a 4/5 shot – 30.2 points, and a possible bet of between £150 and £185, (a loser as it happens).

With the more exotic bets I tend to go level-stakes as specified at the start of the season, depending on the starting size of the fund.

The forecast/exacta element of splitwins, I have on two levels. A normal hit-and-hope £5 combination exacta (total £10) for two outsiders, and £10 combination (total £20) for shorter-priced horses or where I've crossed-out some of the favourites and want to get stuck into the race. This isn't set in stone, but is an easy to follow guideline.

Win doubles I currently do at a minimum £30 to a maximum £60 with £30 a standard stake. £30 is high enough to make sure I've thought about it, and £60 allows me to take advantage of 'saver' doubles when I really think two short-priced horses are going to win. The £60 was set at the start of the season, against a fund size of £12000, - ie half a per cent.

Forecasts/exactas are again on the same two levels - a minimum and standard £5 combination (£30 for 3 horses) to a maximum of £10 (£60 for 3 horses). As I don't do this bet so often, I usually have a good reason (opposing a few short-price uncircled horses), and so tend towards the £60.

Placepot = either 50p or £1 a line.

Each way doubles – between £20 each way and £40 each way.

Placing the bets

Now we can place our bets. Blimey.

We've identified the likely bets in each race based on Racing Post odds, or Pricewise odds. And we've identified our lesser bets – the doubles or placepot etc.

The first thing is to find the best price via Oddschecker, or Teletext. Go through the prices for all your circled horses, putting crosses alongside the ones you can discard on value grounds, and putting the best price, amount of Kelly value and the name of firm alongside the ones representing best value.

Do this for all the races. Then review to see what bets you should be striking, and with whom. One key decision is whether you think that price will be shorter or longer than the declared SP. The best indicators are whether top tipsters (eg Pricewise) have mentioned it or not, and how many newspaper tipsters have tipped it as highlighted in the Tipster box for each meeting.

Personally, if I have decided a horse is value at that price I tend to bet at that price staked to the relevant Kelly points. I'm happy with that value. If the horse does drift I can always go in again. And if any horse drifts markedly from non-value to value I can go in on them also. As it happens I often don't even watch the races live. For example, I go to watch Fulham, and only watch the racing 'as live' on video when I get home.

If between checking the prices and trying to place the bet, the price has shortened, make sure you reduce your bet in line with Kelly value. You've missed out, don't be tempted compound the situation by over-staking. God forbid that you'd actually put more on to make-up for what you've lost. Do that and you've wasted your time reading this far.

You can short-circuit this whole process if early on in the process of study you realise you're going to be keen on something, that it's definitely value, and the price is going tumble. Get on early to a standard half per cent bet, and if need be, or you are able, go in again later at the correct amount. The Royale De Vassey bet would be my example of that, even if I was too slow to get the very best prices.

Chapter 8 – Psychological Aspects

("The next one will be, the next one will be, the next one will be, the next one will be the best one of the year." Alan Price)

So far we've circled horses, looked imaginatively at these horses' chances, worked out a book, compared it with odds available, to identify any value, decided on the right type of bet for the value in the race, and staked an amount on that bet according to our bank. Brilliant. That in itself should mean you bet sensibly and successfully in the long-run.

The one thing left we have to tackle is that unfortunately we are not machines who can treat each bet the same. On any Saturday, I can be affected by all sorts of factors:

- The dull thud of a hangover
- Getting up too late to give myself enough time
- Excitement at an impending Fulham game
- An 'atmosphere' at the breakfast table after an argument with my wife
- Friends coming around, or staying over, limiting my ability to spend time.
- The desire to get some good bets to watch on TV later
- Excitement at the big races (I'm still as excited as I was when I was a kid on Grand National day)
- The knowledge that the fund is struggling and I need a profit from the day
- Excitement that the fund is thriving and a cockiness to get on.

We can look at two overall criteria – firstly our own state of mind, and secondly the shape of the day's racing

Our state of mind

We can look at it in terms of the confidence we have in our approach to that day's gambling. We need to make an assessment. Are we in a good vein of form - in the zone - the horses we're choosing are all running well, and we're making the right decisions about what bets to strike? Or are our horses all falling over – including our flat horses, and we keep on realising after each race that we've actually done the wrong bet, and missed a great value winner. Pick winners? We can't pick our noses. Have we got plenty of time, with no interruptions, to be able to give the day's racing the attention it deserves? Or are we going to be rushing, desperate to get some bets on before having to go Xmas shopping.

The shape of the day's racing

Each Saturday offers a different challenge. Some days there can be three good meetings offering up to twenty possible races to look at. Other Saturdays the racing is quite mediocre (especially weekends before mid-week festivals). At the start of each season you can be faced with loads of half-fit animals. In October, you can be faced with jump racing where you have very little form to go on, and flat racing where half the horses are 'over-the-top' for the season. On the other hand, in the summer months of June, July and August you could have a settled period of weather and a settled period of form. This can be counter-balanced by there being just too much racing for you get your head around it all. You get this dull thrum of overkill. The day may have three really difficult large-field handicaps that will take ages to plough through, or you might come across a jump fixture packed with quality but with only 27 horses spread over 5 races.

We need to have an overall strategy for the day, depending on these factors. Are we going to bet tight, or is this a day we are going to go for it? And we need to know this before we start the whole process. It will make a huge difference to our race selections, our bet selections, our pricing, our determination of value, our bet selection and our staking.

Figure 1 – divides the day's racing in to 4 types. These require differing betting strategies.

Box A: Feeling Good/Racing's Good

It's a great day to be looking at the racing. You're 'in the zone', the circled horses are winning virtually all the races, the ones you're backing are all doing well, the fund's flying. You've got hours to spare, the racing is at your favourite tracks, with nice-sized fields, and you've already noticed a couple of runners you'd love to oppose. We've caught a wave and we need to surf it while it lasts. Your objectives should be:

- To have a go at pricing up all the possible races – this is a good day to be turning over money.
- To be confident about crossing-out horses, so that your circled horses are the real contenders
- To be aggressive in the amount of the book you give to your circled horses.
- To be aggressive in the weight you give to the alternative handicapping factors in pricing up each race
- To stake at the highest multiplier of the Kelly criterion that you're currently using – eg for 6 x Kelly points (rounded up), rather than 5 times.
- To look for some get-rich-quick possibilities – doubles etc
- To be willing stake up to 5% of the fund overall.

Box B: Feeling Bad/Racing's good

Either you are on a losing streak, or you just haven't the time, or right mental attitude to give today's racing your best shot. And that's a real shame because at first sight it looks great. You have happy memories of this weekend from previous years, and one particular race is one of your favourites.

Your objectives should be:

- To isolate quickly which races will be most worthy of your time.
- To be cautious in how you circle horses. If on doubt, leave it in.
- To concentrate on the couple of races where you can see clear value.

- To Stick to win singles and splitwins
- To limit your overall stakes to, at most, 2.5% of fund.

Box C: Feeling good/Racing's bad

You're feeling confident, and eagerly anticipate bashing the bookies like you did last week. Only problem is the going has changed, or it's the wrong time of the year, or it's one of those nothing days prior to a big mid-week meeting, or the racing's so competitive you're going to have 10 circled horses in each race. Be very careful. This is the sort of day that proves the adage 'racing keeps you humble'. This could be where you give it all back to the bookies.

Your objectives should be:

- To make sure you're not going looking for bets in races you would normally avoid.
- To be sensible in circling horses.
- To be sensible in amount of book you award to circled horses
- To think about what alternative handicapping factors could have particular relevance to today's conditions.
- To be imaginative in your bets, looking for the story, and concentrating on bits and pieces bets, (eg placepots) and on outsiders ahead of short-priced single wins and splitwins
- To limit your overall stakes to, at most, 2.5% of fund.

Box D: Feeling bad/ Racing's bad

That 30 bet losing-streak's getting to you, you've got to go and see the in-laws later. Today's the day to leave it well alone. Have a break. Come back refreshed next week.
If you must bet your objectives should be:
- To only choose real races – not the 'possibles'.
- To be very cautious about crossing-out horses
- To be cautious in the amount of book you award to circled horses
- To be careful about being way out of line to the bookies' prices
- To stake the lowest multiplier of the Kelly criterion you currently lose – ie for me Kelly points multiplied by 5 rounded down, rather than by 6.
- To look for sod's law stories, and back them to small stakes (eg saver doubles on the horses you most want to oppose)
- To limit your overall stakes to, at most, 1% of the fund.

Obviously, these represent four extremes. The trick is to decide which box you are in that day, and then decide how strongly you are in it, and amend you overall objectives accordingly. The key is that before you get down to the serious study you have taken a view on whether today you should be betting tight, or betting loose.

Place your bets prior to racing

The above looks at having the right approach to the day's racing as a whole. One problem is that during a day's racing we are going to suffer some amazing highs and lows. We need to be very careful that these don't put us on 'tilt'.

If you've been racing you may recognise the following scenario.

You arrive nice and early and find somewhere to sit, maybe have a drink or have some distinctly dodgy food, and look through the day's racing. Circle some contenders for a fun placepot, and maybe pick out your nap of the day in the third, the one you're going to put a nice wedge on. You've given yourself £100 to play with, hopefully including entrance fee and scoff. In your mind, you've divided it £10 on five races, and £40 or £50 on the big race). Your nap looks to have a lot going for it – Pipe and McCoy, and in this field you may be able to get 4/1. You tell your mates you like the look of that.

You look at the first race and can't see anything you fancy. Two of the big yards have unraced horses with chances – Henrietta Knight and Martin Pipe. You wouldn't dream of betting in this race at home, but as you're here you may as well have a bit of fun. You decide to see what's happening with the prices – they are both a tentative 3/1 on the Racing Post tissue. Opening show has the Pipe horse at 5/2 and Knight's 4/1. You lean towards Henrietta's. After all, you've just seen her and Terry Biddlecombe tucking into fish and chips with the hoi polloi and they looked fairly relaxed. Besides the punters don't give Pipe's a chance and it drifts out to 5/1 at the off. You're happy you got the 'value' (a tenner at 4/1) on the well-backed Knight horse, which goes off at 11/4.

The Pipe horses wins. Knight's drops out of contention three from home. Your placepot choice falls at the last when hanging onto third. You have a drink.

Pipe's got the favourite in the next. It's won it's last two races, looks to be improving and nothing else looks likely. 2/1 will have to do. You'll at least get your money back.

You go outside and it seems everyone wants the Pipe horse. The bookies are being cautious – you see 7/4 a few boards back and try to get there, but a bloke in front of you gets £700 to £400, and the bookie rubs the price off. Most boards are now going 6/4. Suddenly you see 13/8, you run and grab an extra note from your pocket to make the most of it. It's a score. You find yourself giving the bookie both notes. Your tenner fun bet is now a £30 win bet. Still, you're on.

It seems like the whole crowd is on your horse. Two out, it hits the front and the crowd starts cheering. Fantastic. From the corner of your eye you see another horse travelling ominously well a couple of lengths behind. They jump the final flight alongsides and the jockeys settle down to fight it out. Your horse must win under the McCoy drive, but as they stretch away to the line you can see that he other hose is going to win – the cheers die in the crowd's throat. Your mate's girlfriend next to you starts cheering. Her horse Pretty Iris has won at 20/1. "I liked the name" she says. You smile, but you're cross with yourself. And then you look down and see that it was trained by Henrietta Knight. Just brilliant.

The girlfriend gets her £40 winnings from the Tote and buys you all a drink. She's delighted. It's the first time she's been racing and it all seems so simple. You smile. You're a bit late leaving the bar, and the prices are up for the next.

So much for that 4/1. More like 3/1. You groan. You wait to see if it will go to 7/2. You re-look at the form. There's another nice priced

Henrietta Knight horse, this time at 8/1. You look up and see 10/1 at the board next to you. You immediately ask for twenty quid at 10/1. Once you've got your ticket you realise the 'value' on the Pipe horse has gone – it's now 11/4 at best. You go inside and do a fiver combination exacta on the two runners. No, a tenner. After all, you meant to have a good bet on this race.

You go back to the standing area where you and your friends meet between each race. They ask you what price you got. You smile enigmatically and don't say anything. The girl says she's had a fiver on Andrew McCoy. Your friends laugh. And so does she, when AP McCoy goes six lengths clear at the last to win to tumultuous cheers. Knight's horse fell four out when struggling.

You excuse yourself and go the toilet. You go to a cubicle, wondering whether you really are going to pretend to your mates that you had backed the Pipe horse. You count how much money you have left from your hundred. What with a tenner to get in, lunch and a placepot, plus £80 in bets, you have £2.15 left. And it's your round.

Familiar?

You can write your own ending.
- I've borrowed more money off friends to bet with. And lost.
- I've walked off the course after the 4th race without a penny in my pocket
- I've carried on betting via phone accounts and Pipe has continued to lose when backed and win when unbacked.
- I've found a friendly cash machine.
- I've sat in the corner and sulked.

What I haven't ever done is turn it around with a lucky bet in the last. Once you're on tilt you're buggered. As soon as your staking becomes too dependent on your most immediate success or failure you are going to start making some very stupid decisions.

For Saturday gambling, the best thing is to place all your bets on at early prices prior to racing starting. If a horse drifts, and you feel compelled you can always back it again later. There aren't many races, of the kind I bet in, where early prices are unavailable. If you are going to the racecourse I suggest two possible courses of action.

1) Put all your real bets on at early prices before you leave for the course. Any other bets (which you limit to small stakes) are fun 'mug punter' bets such as the girl above is making.
2) Do as above, but allow yourself to take no more than 1% of the fund to the course in case a real betting opportunity arises.

Off-course, you'll still get caught up enough in the day's racing. By far my favourite day's racing is the one where the first bet wins and puts me into profit no matter what happens the rest of the day. I relax and enjoy myself, and in that frame of mind sometimes think I see a nice 'story' bet. If the first few bets lose badly on the other hand, despondency sets in. I suggest neither of these false frames of mind are good times to have a bet. Contain yourself. The only bets wholly allowable during racing are where a horse is drifting and so represents even more value and you should be topping-up your stake. Any time you are about to have a bet during racing challenge yourself

Am I on tilt?

Have other people join the fund

This is one of the best things I've done. They only have a few units, and treat it all as a bit of a laugh, and I recommend it because:

a) It's fun. They phone and get the bets, or you can go racing together, and join in the thrill of a big win. We had a great day out when Compton Admiral won the Coral Eclipse at Sandown at 25/1.

b) They can join in the decision-making. I have final say in all bets in my syndicate – that's because I'm a self-important twat who believes in no-one but himself. It often occurred to me that it would be fascinating to bet with other people doing similar to me, so that we could compare books before we bet.

c) They keep your eyes firmly on the objectives of making money. You have to announce all bets (wherever humanly possible), by phone or e-mail prior to racing. Actually 'proofing' your bets ahead of the races is a magnificent discipline. It means you won't be tempted into ignoring the odd silly loser, or keeping the odd winner to yourself, or otherwise massaging the figures. You also have to provide an end of season summary, detailing all bets, and overall breakdown.

d) It can buy you time – eg from your wife. My wife is an angel at allowing me to spend most Saturdays as I like. She doesn't have a stake in the fund and she often says – 'so what' when I get excited about a winner 'it's nothing to do with me'. So, when I do have the big wins and take a charge on the fund I usually put it towards something for the house, or holiday or night out. We have a lovely set of Le Creuset saucepans that we call the Atone saucepans, bought as they were after his 14/1 success in The Ladbroke hurdle. What's Up Boys bought the Dyson. Bradbury Star a break in Southwold, and so on.

Keep as many notes as possible

In detailing the form of each race as you have done, in your notebooks, you will have far out-stripped virtually every other punter in terms of the amount of note-taking you have made. These notebooks are invaluable.

Each race will detail:

* Your belief as to how competitive it is – circled and % of book
* All the alternative handicapping factors that made the horse a possible bet
* The early morning tissue price
* The percentage per horse you believe to represent value
* The above translated to odds
* The best price available in the morning
* The Kelly value for each horse.
* The bet struck
* The result
* Notes about that race, and about the day as a whole.

Here's an example of a completed notebook entry.

Cheltenham Friday 14th December 2001.

2:20 C handicap hurdle. 2m 1f 10 run 7 circled 85%

Zurs	9/2	6/1	
Benbyas	5/1	6/1	*(7/1 at the off!) 1ˢᵗ F/R*
Kattegat	7/1	15/2	
Tikram	7/1	15/2	*Steamer – 4/1 2nd*
~~Jaguar~~	8/1		

TS	March North	8/1	15/2	£15 @ 10/1
~~TF~~	Misconduct	8/1	10/1	
	~~Present Bleu~~	9/1		
TRC	Fireball Mac	12/1	15/2	£15 @ 10/1

Forecast - £5 combination March North and fireball Macnamara

Incredibly tight handicap. No real alternative factors to play with. Could almost price them all the same. Small bets for fun – no proper value.

Benbyas drifted to a backable price. I also wish with hindsight I'd noted the jockey booking of Dobbin, that may have made me price it tighter and made me strike bet.

Fireball Macnamara drifted to 14/1 Had another tenner.

All comments not in bold were written prior to the race. The comments on bold were added after the race. You'll find this builds up to into a wealth of information. Looking back at previous year's notes about the equivalent meeting is often a good reminder about how competitive the meeting can be etc.

It's also useful to generate 'reminders' or 'rules' from the notebook comments to help you in the future. Here's some of the recent ones I've made:

- Whenever betting one of two horses with same trainer, and the one you're betting is the longest of the two – do the forecast.
- Make sure the percentages look right. If you find you've got a lot of value bets (eg 3), and you're not obviously opposing anything, you've priced it up wrong

- Just because a horse doesn't have any alternative handicapping factors, doesn't necessarily mean it can't be a hot favourite, (if not odds on?)
- Always, always forgive one run.
- Don't let absences put you off if trainer is in form
- Hennessey – last year. Kingsmark, Beau and Foxchapel King, all ran a good speed rating on bad ground 2 weeks before. That is an insufficient period of time to recover from a fast race on bad ground.
- Venetia Williams talks of handicapper putting horses up the handicap quickly. She says she'll be aiming unexposed horses straight at big prizes, rather than running up a sequence.
- Ratings accounting for weight are skewed. A top-rated top-weight has an even better chance than it looks, and a top-rated low-weight has a lesser chance.
- Generally, do more forecasts – to small stakes if need be.
- Three or more alternative handicapping pointers is notable. Two negative pointers (and no positive) can lead you to 'uncircle' a horse.

And that's about it folks. Give it a go and let me know how you get on.

And good luck!

(Notes 2016)

Blimey this book reads like something from the historical archives. 2001 really was a different country. "If you have a PC" – we're nearly at the stage where PCs themselves have come and gone!

It also mentions flutter.com. This was the original Betfair and the prominence of Betfair has done more than most to change betting.

Anyway, let's look at what's different and what's the same.

You still need a dedicated betting bank.

You still need as many betting accounts as you can open. On the plus side there are now even more betting companies to sign up with, all of them competing with each other to get your business. If you take advantage of all their offers, you'll probably be something like a grand up in free bets to get you started. On the down side, I no longer have a lot of these accounts. One thing you should know is that, if you are any good, a lot of these companies are going to restrict your account or close it down. I could go off on one at this juncture and I probably do on my website somewhere, but for now let's just say open as many accounts as you can, and if you do get restricted or closed down I'd suggest wearing that as a badge of honour.

There's a lot of stuff (free or subscription) online these days and I doubt you need to buy the Racing Post every day. I don't, but I do subscribe online. And these days every race is shown live on TV – neither Racing UK or At The Races existed when this book was written.

Choosing which races to bet in

You still need to narrow down which races to bet in – to specialise to some degree. However, I'd disregard everything here and do your own thing. I say that because my own choices have changed totally since I wrote the book. These days I specialise in novice hurdles and novice chases, plus play at courses I know and like and understand, and that have been profitable for me in the past (Cheltenham, Sandown, Epsom...) I still play in one or two of the big races on the big occasions, but mainly for the fun.

Shortlisting horses

This is clearly based on class 3 or higher racing. Many of the comments do not apply to lower levels, so beware. As a simplistic guide to form it works ok.

Alternative factors

The key thing I'm trying to get across here, is there's loads of angles into races. All of the things mentioned are potential edges and most of them remain so. Personally, I find myself having come full circle and am back studying trainers as closely as I ever have done. The thing is, you need to do your own work. Choose a potential angle and get digging.

Research your own stats, collect lists of horses running well from bad draws, compile your own trends for particular races, follow a trainer closely until you can predict where and why they are going to place particular horses, become a time guru, or a pace guru – whatever gives you a way into the race that may throw it into a new shape and one not fully accounted for in the prices available.

Or, be more like me, and use a shallower scattergun approach across many of these factors depending on the type of race, time of year, track, whatever.

And there is one great new tool that was barely available when I wrote the book. Yep, the internet. Sure, it's the wild west stuffed full of charlatans, trolls and bug-eyed lunatics. But it's also amazing for picking up free information. Get reading, get searching, join forums, follow people on twitter, you'll be inundated with mini angles and systems and free tips and requests for money.

Obviously, you need to navigate your way through it all, separate the wheat from the chaff, and ideally you need to be looking for stuff beneath the radar, that isn't already affecting the prices. But believe me, there's a load of great stuff out there. Who knows, some of it might be worth paying for, not that I recommend this.

Pricing Races

This reads OK. To be honest pricing up races comes so automatically to me these days it's almost as though I don't do it at all – I can already see which horses I think will be too short and which too long. But as a simple (or simplistic) introduction to pricing events up it seems to work.

One thing I would say:
Bookmakers aren't as driven by over-round as they used to be. In fact, with tight margins they are often betting very close to 100% - on uncompetitive small field races and Premiership football matches for example. And certainly, taking best prices across all the bookmakers on oddschecker, they are often close to 100%. They've been driven to do this through competition, and not least through the need to compete with Betfair, who are essentially always working to around 100% (plus commission), regardless of field size.

You'd think this would be a disaster for them, but actually it doesn't seem to be. If they can weed out the disciplined punters betting only at the very best prices – by limiting or closing down their accounts – then they still have three great weaknesses on their side.

- People who don't shop around for best prices
- People who want some action – on every race
- People who stake inconsistently (play up their winnings, chase their losses).

Finding Value

I'm not sure I've got anything to say about this, except I might have been asking the wrong question, or failing to ask the right question. Patrick Veitch – well-known professional gambler – probably put his finger on it in his book when he said the key question as to whether something is value or not is finding the answer to the following question.

Why might the prices be wrong?

If you can answer that, then you're onto something, and probably not just on this event or race. Probably you're onto something more fundamental. Potentially a systematic pricing area that plays across lots of events and markets. There's some examples at the end.

What sort of race are you looking at?

Before finding the right bet, I would add a new thought – what sort of race are you looking at?

I think in terms of five main types, as decided on by the number of circled horses:

Legitimate favourite races

Either the only horse circled or a horse seemingly well-clear of the others. Remember the idea of placing those world cup teams into post of varying degrees of chances – a legitimate fave is in a pot of its own.

Co-Choice races

Only two horses circled or two horses well clear of the rest and very close on form.

"Play" races

4 or 5 horses with chances, none of them clear, or possibly one of them a favourite you think is very beatable for some reason and accordingly a rotten price.

Competitive races

5 or more horses with legitimate chances.

Unfathomable races

you can't get a handle on the race – form is erratic or non-existent, or there's too many unexposed horses taking part. Whatever, avoid like the plague. There's always another race.

These race types can be combined. For example, you can have a competitive race but, even so, it's got a legitimate favourite, which you've put in a pot by itself clear of all the challengers.

Once you've sorted out what type of race you've got, you can then consider why the prices might be wrong. Take a co-choice race, with only two legitimate contenders.

One of the horses is ridden by the champion jockey who has gone to the course for one ride for a major trainer. The other is trained by a small stable and ridden by an unfashionable jockey. Their form chance is pretty much identical. You have priced them up as co-faves. But which one is actually going to be fave and which one is going to be "value"?

Here's how I would tend to bet these days in each type of race, assuming the price is right.

Legitimate fave – single win bet on fave – with possibly a saver on something else.

Co-choice – outsider of the two – single win, if seems value.

Play races – possibly split-wins on two or more runners, possibly including a saver, but probably opposing the fave for some reason.

Competitive - looking for outsiders, particularly each way at attractive odds, and especially with enhanced place terms. Forecasts also. Possible saver on legitimate fave.

Why Might the Prices be Wrong?

Here's some ideas. They overlap; some are general and some specific so inevitably some are subsets of others.

The markets are difficult for odds compilers to price up well due to lack of knowledge or similar.
a) The Big Brother markets in the early days – no-one had a clue – on the first night you could arb all evening on different prices. Three years in and the prices were 'accurate' within 20 minutes of the end of the first show.
b) The place market is very complicated to get a handle on. There will be some people with very accurate prices but the suspicion remains that the win market prices continue to have too much influence on the place prices.
c) The odds compiler is running a market they are not expert in – minor sports or leagues do not have the same dedicated expertise as mainstream sports.

Changing circumstances
a) change of going prior to a meeting or race
b) anticipating the eventual make-up of a race ante post and its effect on prices (eg changing each way terms, likely non runners)
c) form within meetings – eg trainer/jockey form; draw and pace bias, mounting liabilities from jockey doubles/trebles.

Balancing Books/Managing Liabilities
a) the initial prices are broadly right, but a late steamer causes other prices to lengthen.
b) balancing in-running books – eg a league title book – where bookies may make a short-term conscious decision to get a team in the satchel simply to do a bit of internal accounting.

Overreaction to one negative or positive
a) A horse is carrying a penalty and it will be difficult to win with it.
Plenty of commentators have mentioned this and the vibes are bad.
No-one wants to back it, and plenty of part-timers want to lay it. It
drifts to a big price. But the initial price had already at least partly
discounted its chances on the basis of that factor.
b) team news in football.
c) jockey changes

Rumours creating bullish or bearish market reactions
a) Football manager markets!

Bias
a) Patriotism
b) big team bias and big trainer bias, and overlooking small teams
and small stables
b) lady jockeys
c) Popular horses/golfers etc who haven't really got their conditions
in this event but people want to 'support' anyway, (and odds
compilers are aware of this).

Chaos – usually caused by volatility in-running when odds compilers
struggle to keep up with the changes and ascertain true prices.
a) all in-running sports

Greed – betting against the people desperate to win at any odds
a) in-running the general rule is an over anticipation of success and
a tendency to chase prices down too far.
b) illiquid markets offer opportunities to encourage impatient
people to take poor prices.

Over-reaction/Under-reaction to either the facts or the potential.
a) overrated – what a horse may achieve; under-rated what it has
already achieved
b) Overrated - a horse that wins a big race as well-backed favourite.

c) recency effect - underrated - a horse that fails when a short price for a big race – now scorned by punters talking through their pockets - "always forgive a horse one failure".
d) overrated – the last couple of performances of a football team

Popularity
a) Jockeys, horses, trainers, owners, over-bet and priced accordingly, compared to jockeys, trainers, horses under-bet.
b) Trainers – the big names at unfashionable courses will always be put in short – conservatively and if they're not you should be asking yourself why not. Gambling stables will be priced conservatively and adjust according to whether the money is coming. Keep a list of trainers/owners whose horses drift late and never win and those who contract late and never lose.
c) Some horses are sexy horses and over-bet accordingly.
d) Some horses, particularly late improvers, the public take time to forgive past transgressions.
e) Personally, I believe horses with impossible to pronounce or spell names are under-bet.
f) Also, horses lower down the race-card are under-et compared to those higher up the race-card. Foreign horses are often under-bet.
g) A jockey – Ryan Moore with a good book of rides at a middling course, say - will find all his mounts priced up conservatively early on – to account for all those Yankees etc. How those prices drift or stay strong as the day progresses is a good indicator of strength behind each individual horse.

Snowball effect/Groupthink
There's a weak novice hurdle. A horse with a string of seconds to its name is well clear on ratings and should be Evens at least. You don't like it much – you suspect it's a dog – and this is clear in formbook comments and in the Racing Post, whatever. The bookies themselves are likely to want to take it on a bit and will have priced this into their early morning prices. Through the day, the noise surrounding the horse gathers momentum, tipsters on the racing

channel and so on, all say they would rather be a layer than a player, without ever really coming up with a credible alternative. A couple of other horses are shortening but not aggressively. Or they say they'd rather sit and watch at the price. The starting price is eventually an uneasy 6/4 or even 7/4. What price do you think was right?

Um, that's about it. As I finish writing this update the son of a friend I have been helping with his gambling messaged me with a screenshot of his William Hill account, showing me that it is 4 figures to the good after yet another win on a football-based system I gave him earlier this year. (I am sitting here wondering why I am currently not following this system myself!) He's sending me a nice bottle of 10 year old tawny port as thanks – or at least he better be. And if anyone else profits from anything in this book please feel free to do the same.

I'm made up for him and I hope he gets as much enjoyment out of gambling over the years as I have. At the same time the four runner novice chase I bet on this morning has just finished. I dutched the 2nd and 3rd faves against the fave, and have just watched the complete outsider win instead. This is somewhat typical of how my year has been. You've been warned.

So, I guess I'll sign off by repeating what a dear old syndicate friend said to me many years ago. "I think we should be putting more on the ones that win and less on the ones that lose. In fact, thinking about it, I'm not sure why we're putting anything on the ones that lose at all."

Good luck.